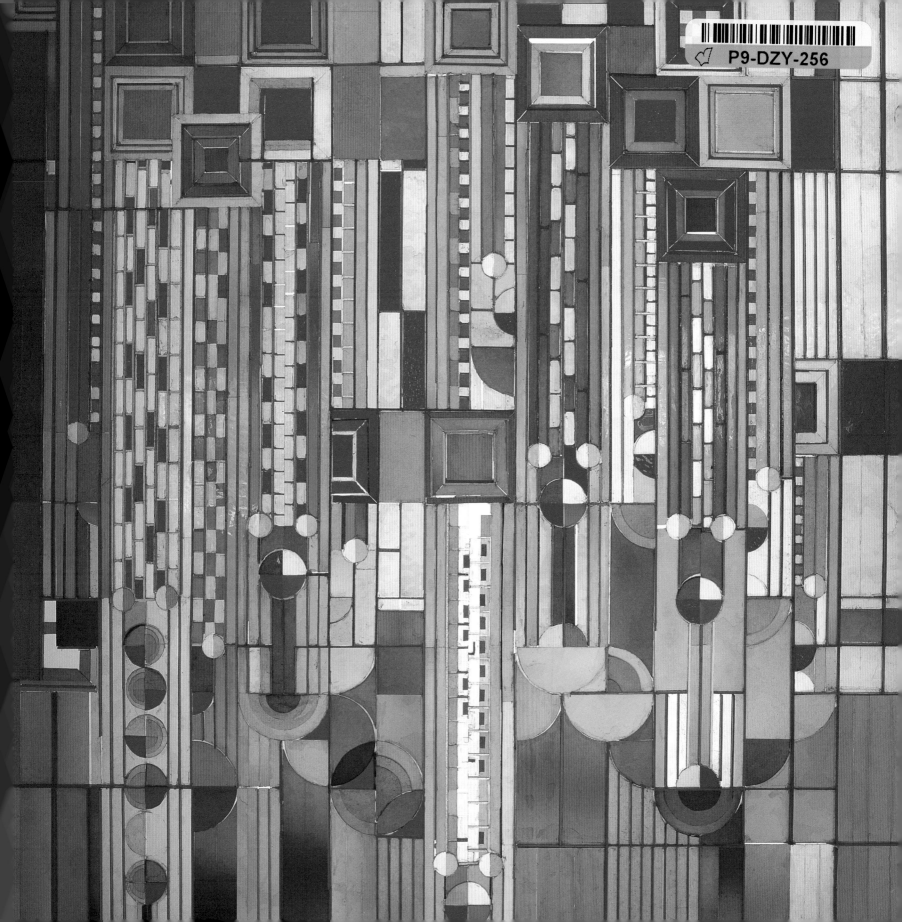

FRANK LLOYD WRIGHT:
THE WESTERN WORK

FRANK LLOYD WRIGHT: THE WESTERN WORK

By **DIXIE LEGLER**
Photographs by **SCOT ZIMMERMAN**
Introduction by **ARTHUR DYSON**

CHRONICLE BOOKS
SAN FRANCISCO

Endsheets: (front) Taliesin West, Arizona Biltmore, Price Residence; (back) Pottery House, Arizona Biltmore, Blair Residence

Page 2: Frank Lloyd Wright at Taliesin West, 1947.

Text copyright © 1999 by Dixie Legler.
Photographs copyright © 1999 by Scot Zimmerman.
Introduction copyright © 1999 by Arthur Dyson.

Photographs on pages 2, 6, 12, 48, and 49 copyright © 1999 by Pedro E. Guerrero.

Drawings and photographs on pages 9 (right), 11, 33, 71, and 141 courtesy of the Frank Lloyd Wright Foundation, © 1999.

Library of Congress Cataloging-in-Publication Data available.

ISBN 0-8118-1785-7

Printed in Hong Kong.

Designed and typeset by Anne Galperin

Distributed in Canada by Raincoast Books
8680 Cambie Street
Vancouver, British Columbia V6P 6M9

10 9 8 7 6 5 4 3 2 1

Chronicle Books
85 Second Street
San Francisco, California 94105

www.chroniclebooks.com

ACKNOWLEDGMENTS

This book is dedicated to our dear friend and colleague Pedro E. Guerrero, whose work with Frank Lloyd Wright and joy in life are a constant inspiration. We are also grateful to the following individuals, who generously opened their homes or offered assistance: Gail Baker, Ruth and Quintin Blair, the Rev. William Boice, Dr. William and Ann Brennan, Dr. David Carlquist, Janet Cooper and the U-Haul Corporation, Jack Cullen and Deborah Vick, Alan Davis, George Frandsen, Frank Gregg, Mark Griggs, Mrs. Charles Kinter, Delton Ludwig, Philip McClanahan, Linda Melton, Alex Pappas, Christian Petersen, Chuck and Melinda Roland, E. Soiero, Donald and Jane Stromquist, William and Elizabeth Tracy, and Alice Urban. From the Frank Lloyd Wright Foundation we thank Bruce Brooks Pfeiffer, Margo Stipe, Oscar Muñoz, Suzette Lucas, Penny Fowler, Frank Henry, Indira Berndtson, Charles Montooth, John Rattenbury, and E. Thomas Casey. Special recognition goes to Arthur Dyson for his insightful introduction; to William LeBlond, Judith Dunham, and Alan Rapp of Chronicle Books for their guidance; and to Ann Zimmerman and John Legler for their invaluable help and encouragement.

DIXIE LEGLER
SCOT ZIMMERMAN

CONTENTS

The West offered Wright a rich laboratory of materials and endless possibilities for new building forms. For the Rose Pauson House, his first residential commission in Arizona, he scooped up rocks from the desert floor to form the masonry supports and used redwood and glass for the upper walls. Designed in 1939, the house was ravaged by fire two years later.

INTRODUCTION
by ARTHUR DYSON

AS AN APPRENTICE OF FRANK LLOYD WRIGHT in his final years, I learned firsthand of his love for the West. The magical creation of Taliesin West, his winter home in Arizona, remains a magnificent indication of how deeply Mr. Wright was moved by an environment so different from the context of his earlier works. His organic theory of architectural design found opportunities for entirely new forms of expression that would flow through the course of the decades in his later life.

The lure of the West was an opportunity for Mr. Wright to channel new energies into innovative building techniques with a fresh palette of materials. Experiments with structures that could capture the songs of nature and embrace the outdoors beyond anything possible in eastern climes now became a reality. Windows and doors were arranged to inform a unified movement of mind and body, creating a continuum of experiential space from inside to outside. The feeling of separation between these places becomes nearly non-existent, allowing an unprecedented architectonic freedom of living.

Although primarily known for his midwestern works, Mr. Wright conceived buildings in all the western states: Arizona, Idaho, Montana, Oregon, Utah, Washington, Wyoming, and California. The western work spanned five decades, from 1909 to 1959 (the year of his death), and several of the works designed during this period were posthumously built, such as First Christian Church, Grady Gammage Memorial Auditorium, and the Jester-Pfeiffer Residence. Tragically, some of the other works no longer exist, among them Como Orchards clubhouse and most of the cottages, Bitter Root Inn, the Rose Pauson house, several Biltmore cottages, Ocatilla (his first desert complex), Shelter-in-the-Wash, and Sun Trap.

With the exception of the Montana oeuvres, Mr. Wright's western work largely represents his "second career" period after the 1920s. By the time he was in his sixties, his creative output had slowed down considerably; so little of his production between 1923 and 1934 was seen by the public that many assumed he had died. By the time his work once again claimed wide attention, his outlook had become invigorated by his life in the West.

Mr. Wright loved the climate, the cool mornings and searing afternoons of the Arizona desert, and was drawn to the organic life that dwelled therein. He was mesmerized by the practical beauty of the saguaro, calling the cactus a "perfect example of reinforced construction. . . . A truer skyscraper than we have yet built. And all these remarkable desert growths show economy in their patterns of construction; the stalks especially teach any architect or engineer who is modest and intelligent enough to apply for lessons."

In Arizona especially, the climate was amenable to designs that produced conditions of comfort by natural means. Buildings varied necessarily in materials and siting to suit their surroundings, yet there was a constancy of what he called "grammar."

LEFT Perched atop a promontory near Wright's Boomer and Adelman Houses in Phoenix, this simple rubblestone chimney is all that remains of the Pauson House.

RIGHT Wright found great inspiration in the desert vegetation, particularly the saguaro cactus, which he regarded as a natural skyscraper. The thirteen cabins of his 1928-29 desert encampment, Ocatilla, near Chandler, Arizona, overlooked several spectacular specimens.

Mr. Wright often spoke of the relevance of grammar in a building—an active part of his theories since the early 1900s. He would emphasize the importance of "shape-relationship" between the various parts of any composition. "The grammar of a house," he explained, "is its manifest articulation of all its parts. This will be the 'speech' it uses." The southwestern desert provided, and indeed insisted on, a different vocabulary than he had employed before.

With the latitude to experiment in new materials, for example, came the architectonic use of canvas, both as an easily movable covering and a light diffuser. Use of this fabric, especially in conjunction with openings, blossomed into a principal structural experience of light and air. "If one may have air and feel the current of air moving in one's face and hands and feet, one can take almost any degree of heat," he said. "It is best to have a thorough protection overhead and the rest of the building as open to breezes as it possibly can be made." Air circulation, therefore, became a prime design consideration to provide natural cooling without mechanical air conditioning.

Several factors motivated Mr. Wright to migrate West. One, of course, was to escape the severe

northern winters and costly heating bills of his Wisconsin home, Taliesin. In terms of building, the humid summers, severe winter blizzards, temperature ranges among the seasons that cause structural materials to expand and contract, torrential rains, damaging hailstones and heavy frosts that were commonplace in the Midwest were mitigated or nonexistent in the West. Projects such as San Marcos-in-the-Desert, Ocatilla, Oasis (the proposed Arizona State Capitol), and Taliesin West celebrated this sense of liberation. While the majority of the western works would be designed for Arizona, the beginnings of the move lay elsewhere.

In 1909 Mr. Wright received his first commission in the West outside of California, but various financial disasters would hamper his first endeavors there. This opportunity took the form of a master plan for Como Orchards, also known as University Heights, consisting of a clubhouse, land office building, and cottages in the Bitter Root Valley of Montana After twelve cottages and a two-story clubhouse were built, financial problems caused bank foreclosure in 1916. The cottages were demolished in the late 1930s, and the clubhouse went down in 1945. The Bitter Root Valley Irrigation Company also commissioned him to design a town plan and a hotel, but after the Bitter

Root Inn was erected in 1909, the company's subsequent bankruptcy terminated all other development. The building was used as a school, and later as a dance hall, until the structure burned in 1924.

After other personal and legal setbacks left Mr. Wright "homeless and about penniless," entailing foreclosure and eviction from his beloved Taliesin, he received a telegram from Albert McArthur in 1928. McArthur was the son of a former client and personal friend, a draftsman from the Oak Park studio some twenty years earlier. The telegram was an invitation asking his help with a hotel that McArthur was planning in partnership with his brothers, the Biltmore Hotel in Phoenix, Arizona.

Although the actual role played by Mr. Wright in the design of the Biltmore is still a subject of dispute, he worked on the project "incognito and behind the scenes" for nine months. During construction, the multitude of alterations by "consultants" and compromises in the structural system later caused him to disown the work. As Mr. Wright explained, "The building was finally built, but meanwhile encountered the inevitable opposition to the unusual in design and new in construction. Albert was totally unable to stem the collateral tides of suggested changes which experts and engineers proposed in my building technique." Perhaps it is true that Mr. Wright's diluted vision and McArthur's compromises in the design were the premise for Ayn Rand's *The Fountainhead.*.

An acquaintance made through his work at the Biltmore, however, launched Mr. Wright's own desert works. While working on the hotel, McArthur introduced him to Dr. Alexander Chandler. This veterinarian-turned-developer invited him to design a luxury desert resort hotel, San Marcos-in-the-Desert. Mr. Wright wrote, "there could be nothing more inspiring to an architect on this earth than this spot of pure Arizona desert." He completed the first design sketches while living in La Jolla, California, finishing them in mid 1929, by which time he was living on-site with a fifteen-member entourage and his family. The land, overlooking the proposed resort location, was provided by Dr. Chandler, and the camp complex itself—Ocatilla—presaged Taliesin West in its desert-adapted design and materials. The venting canvas triangles in gable ends were painted scarlet, similar to the flowering desert plant called ocotillo ("candle flame"), hence the name, which Mr. Wright misspelled variously as "Ocatillo" or "Ocatilla."

After completed drawings for San Marcos were delivered, a $480,000 construction contract was signed. While samples of beautiful cross-grained concrete block stood waiting at the Ocatilla Camp, and with Chandler en route to sign the contract, news of the stock market crash came—the project was immediately killed. Mr. Wright collected only $2,500 of his $40,000 fee, and he returned to Wisconsin in May. In July, half of the camp burned and the desert and many of its human occupants eventually reclaimed what was left behind.

Had it been built, San Marcos-in-the-Desert would have been among his most innovative projects. He once told me that the San Marcos presentation drawing done by his son Lloyd was the most beautiful rendering he had ever seen. "The building was . . . too good to be true," Mr. Wright remembered. "I have found that when a scheme develops beyond a normal pitch of excellence, the hand of fate strikes it down. The Japanese made a superstition of the circumstance. Purposely they leave some imperfection somewhere to appease the jealousy of the gods. I neglected this precaution. San Marcos was not built."

The experience was still fruitful. The camps that were meant as temporary housing for Mr. Wright, his family, and his associates, allowed him to further develop a grammar suitable for the desert. Several years earlier, in 1927, Mr. Wright had designed the Ras-El-Bar Vacation Cabins, built in Damiette, Egypt, and featuring tentlike structures of wood and canvas set on concrete slabs. Canvas emerged again as a material that would open up new possibilities of building and living in the desert climate. He once wrote, "the white luminous canvas overhead and canvas used instead of window glass

afforded such an agreeable diffusion of light within, was so enjoyable and sympathetic to the desert, that I now felt much more than ever oppressed by the thought of the opaque solid overhead of the much too heavy Midwestern house."

Mr. Wright extended this vocabulary to another design for Dr. Chandler, the San Marcos Water Gardens, using canvas roofing and concrete walls. But this and other promising Chandler commissions would run their ultimately disappointing courses, and none were built. The first was the San Marcos Polo Stables and Golf Clubhouse in late 1929, an expansion and alteration to the existing San Marcos Hotel in downtown Chandler. The final two projects were drafted in 1936: Little San Marcos Resort Inn, a much more modest version of the great resort designed seven years earlier, and an extensive

The Ocatilla cabins were made of simple materials, primarily wood and canvas. Inside, however, Wright did not stint. Even in this desert site, without running water or electricity, he provided space for what he regarded as life's "necessities": a grand piano and a lavish display of Native American rugs. Wright, his family, and a small band of draftsmen worked and lived in these cabins while preparing drawings for San Marcos-in-the-Desert.

Always impeccably dressed with his trademark porkpie hat,
Wright ponders a design problem in 1952.

remodeling of Dr. Chandler's San Marcos Hotel, their last joint collaboration.

Although the stability of his work suffered severely during the mid- to late 1920s and early 1930s, Mr. Wright was far from inactive. Many later projects had early connections to work in the western states. In 1931, he designed the Capital Journal building in Salem, Oregon, which was supported on reinforced hollow concrete piers with lily pad tops—the prototype for the Johnson Wax building some five years later. The "House on the Mesa" was exhibited in the International Exhibition of Modern Architecture held at the Museum of Modern Art in 1932 to great acclaim. Taliesin West and the Kaufmann House—

better known as the famous Fallingwater, in western Pennsylvania—both owe much to this project.

Returning to Arizona for two winter stays at Dr. Chandler's La Hacienda, every Sunday he would picnic in the surrounding areas searching for a building site for Taliesin West. In late 1937, he found approximately 800 acres on the Maricopa Mesa at the base of the McDowell Mountains, near Scottsdale, which he purchased complete with water rights. In the spring of 1938, the first structure, Shelter-in-the-Wash, was built, consisting of a root cellar, kitchen, dining area, and drafting room. Also in 1938 Sun Trap—living quarters for Mr. Wright, his wife, Olgivanna, and their daughter, Iovanna—was constructed. Shelter-in-the-Wash was dismantled in 1938 after the permanent buildings were raised. Sun Trap was likewise rebuilt for his daughter, into a cottage known as Sun Cottage.

With little outside help, thirty-five apprentices built Taliesin West over the course of seven winters. Additions and alterations continued until Mr. Wright's death in 1959 (and afterwards). Arizona winters allowed Mr. Wright and the fellowship an opportunity to enjoy the outdoors during winter, something the northern climates denied. The desert setting provided an abundance of sunburned flat rocks and sand for concrete, and Mr. Wright designed a new form of construction fitted to the unskilled labor of the apprentices. Rather than import stonemasons from Wisconsin, he devised a type of masonry never before seen, using the flat, colorful stones in the formwork, and pouring desert-mixed cement into wooden forms to bind them.

In a poetic stream of vision, Taliesin West was evoked: "The plans were inspired by the character and beauty of that wonderful site," Mr. Wright said. "But for the designing of our buildings certain forms abounded. They were simple characteristic silhouettes to go by, tremendous drifts and heaps of sunburned desert rocks were nearby to be used. We got it all together within the landscape—where God is all and man is naught—as a more permanent extension of 'Ocatilla,' the first canvas-topped desert camp of Architecture by youthful enthusiasm for posterity to ponder."

From the Como Orchards clubhouse of 1909 to the Lykes house in 1959, seamless passage of architectural style is evident in diverse aspects. The plans range from circles to triangles to squares. Materials vary from wood to steel to stone to concrete to canvas (the luminescent quality of the latter changing his outlook significantly). Clerestories and skylights became the norm rather than the exception, blossoming perfectly into even industrial-scale works like the Johnson Wax Administration Building.

This book presents twenty-three works of astounding diversity. These contrast with earlier works by Mr. Wright in the East and Midwest, and include hotels, private homes, Usonian Automatics (Pieper, Tracy, and Adelman), several radial or circular plans (including one for his son David Wright), low-cost housing (Carlson), a church (First Christian, part of the unrealized Christian University), a medical clinic (Lockridge Clinic), a performing arts auditorium (Grady Gammage), and several cottages (Como Orchards and Arizona Biltmore). Within the variety found among these designs, there is, of course, the inevitable distinction of Frank Lloyd Wright's work. All these designs share the inspired commonality of genius that makes them recognizable works of the master.

For this present work, take the descriptions of Dixie Legler and the masterful photographs by Scot Zimmerman as your guide. Many of you will encounter these structures for the first time. Others will discover different perspectives and new insights about their backgrounds. In the words of Frank Lloyd Wright, "Only when the buildings are comprehended from within and each in its place, a feature of its own special environment—serving its own appropriate purpose with integrity—are they really seen." This book is a very fine letter of introduction.

COMO ORCHARDS SUMMER COLONY

1909 DARBY, MONTANA

IN A REMOTE AREA of western Montana, a broad valley stretches between the dagger-sharp Bitter Root Range and the softly rounded Sapphire Mountains. Where mountain meets valley, apples still hang from the gnarled branches of a few ancient fruit trees, a poignant reminder of the once prosperous orchards that dotted the Montana countryside in the early 1900s. The "Apple Boom," which lasted in the Bitter Root Valley until 1920, lured big investors and big names to the region, including Frank Lloyd Wright, who designed two town plans, a recreation community, and several buildings in the heart of apple country. Only two small cottages remain of the fourteen Wright-designed buildings that were constructed here. Both have been substantially altered.

Montana's climate and long growing season were judged ideal for apple production at the turn of the twentieth century, but irrigation was sorely needed to supplement the region's meager rainfall. By 1910, an ambitious eighty-mile-long irrigation canal, known locally as the "Big Ditch," channeled water from Lake Como to the entire length of the Bitter Root Valley, nourishing thousands of acres of trees. Two Chicago businessmen, W. I. Moody and Frederick D. Nichols, were the principal leaders of the Bitter Root Valley Irrigation Company, which built the multimillion-dollar canal project. They hoped to recoup the company's substantial investment by selling water to orchard owners and attracting investors in the apple-growing business.

LEFT This three-bedroom board-and-batten dwelling was one of fifty-eight rustic cabins designed by Wright for the Como Orchards Summer Colony in the mountains of western Montana. Cruciform in plan with a low hipped roof, the cabin has been greatly altered since 1909.

RIGHT Wright specified natural fieldstone for the fireplace and instructed it to be laid with deep mortar joints, but he would recognize little else of his design in the interior of this three-bedroom cabin.

Their first endeavor was the sixteen-hundred-acre Como Orchards Summer Colony, for which they turned to prominent Chicago architect Frank Lloyd Wright. The plan—also known as University Heights because its major investors were university professors—called for fifty-eight cottages to be arranged around a central clubhouse, with tennis courts, a cascading fountain, and a natural pond completing the scene. Wright traveled to Montana in February of 1909 at the invitation of Moody and Nichols to inspect the site.

The cabins in Wright's plan were of three basic designs ranging from one to four rooms, with several variations. Each was to have a rustic feel tempered with typical Wright touches: bands of casement windows, deep sheltering eaves, French doors, hipped roofs, natural fieldstone fireplaces, and horizontal board-and-batten siding. Most lacked kitchens since the inhabitants were expected to take their meals in the clubhouse, an expansive two-story inn that anchored Wright's plan. The clubhouse, also of horizontal board and batten, was cruciform in plan with a low hipped roof, a two-story central lounge, three fieldstone fireplaces, and a long bank of tall windows overlooking the spectacular Sapphire Mountains to the east and hundreds of acres of apple orchards. Excluding the porte cocheres that flanked the structure, the clubhouse stretched out 164 feet northeast to southwest on a gently sloping site.

Designed to appeal to the "eastern elite," the scheme lured dozens of professors, particularly from the University of Chicago. They were encouraged to purchase ten-acre lots in the apple orchard for $400 an acre, which also included a building site for a summer cabin. Between 1909 and 1910, the clubhouse, a

This smaller cabin, which once served as the land office, nestles into a deep wooded ravine on the northern edge of the entrance drive. Its hipped roof, deep porch, wood-mullioned windows, and board-and-batten siding offer a faint glimpse of Wright's original plans for the project.

sales office, and eleven cabins were built, none exactly according to Wright's specifications.

Shortly after completing the design for Como Orchards, Wright was enlisted by the Bitter Root Valley Irrigation Company for a second, more ambitious project. Wright was to lay out the new town of Bitter Root, envisioned by its backers to someday outrank Missoula in population and importance. The main objective, again, was the apple business and courting investors who would settle in Bitter Root to tend to their trees. Wright was also asked to design several buildings, only one of which, the Bitter Root Inn, was constructed. Built in 1910, the 126-foot-long board-and-batten inn was a sweeping structure with a low gabled roof, specially patterned windows, and a wide veranda with views of Harriet Park to the west.

The new town of Bitter Root, located about thirty miles from Como Orchards at the northern end of the Big Ditch, was an early attempt by Wright at city planning. Laid out in a geometric grid, the plan featured thirteen square blocks, each with a central courtyard. Most impressive was an ambitious two-level transportation system that included a depressed rail line. But Wright's scheme for this mountain town was not adopted, nor was a second plan he proposed. Although water and power were brought to the site, only a handful of buildings were constructed. In 1924, the Bitter Root Inn, which had served time as a dance hall, burned to the ground.

The Como Orchards Summer Colony suffered a similar fate. A devastating blight nearly wiped out all the valley's orchards in 1913 and, coupled with a federal lawsuit and escalating shipping costs, drove the company to bankruptcy in 1916. In 1923, new owners of Como Orchards renamed the business McIntosh-Morello Orchards, whitewashed the clubhouse, and converted it into a packing hall and bunkhouse. That endeavor failed too, and in 1945 the clubhouse was dismantled. All but two of the cottages were destroyed, leaving little in this area of Montana to recall Wright's contribution to the state.

Arizona Biltmore, viewed from the south. Though Albert Chase McArthur is the credited with the layout of the hotel, in its character, detail, and intricate geometry it clearly reflects the work of Frank Lloyd Wright, who served as a consultant. A perforated copper roof folds over the upper floor, throwing light and shadow over the facade. Seventeen tons of copper and a quarter-million precast concrete blocks form the core of the building.

ARIZONA BILTMORE

1927 PHOENIX, ARIZONA

THE ARIZONA BILTMORE, romantic and mysterious, holds a secret within its elegant walls. No one is certain who is responsible for this gracious landmark. Was it Frank Lloyd Wright, whose hand is so evident in the skillful detailing? Or was it Albert Chase McArthur, the architect of record, who hired Wright to consult on the project? At times Wright claimed a vital role: "Albert had a plan for the building that was impracticable. . . . So we threw it all away and started again." At other times he gave McArthur credit: "Albert McArthur is the architect of that building. All attempts to take the credit for that performance from him are gratuitous and beside the mark." Today historians generally credit McArthur with the overall layout and preliminary plan, but attribute many of the details of the hotel and the design of the guest cottages to Wright. A set of six conceptual sketches in the Frank Lloyd Wright Archives testifies to his critical involvement. Whatever Wright's true role, his arrival in Phoenix in January, 1928, was a pivotal moment in his life and career. For without this commission and the contacts he made during his stay, a score of other Wright designs for the desert, including his own home, Taliesin West, might never have been realized.

Building a resort hotel in Phoenix was the brainchild of Albert McArthur's brothers, Warren and Charles McArthur, who prophetically envisioned that the area would someday be a mecca for winter tourists.

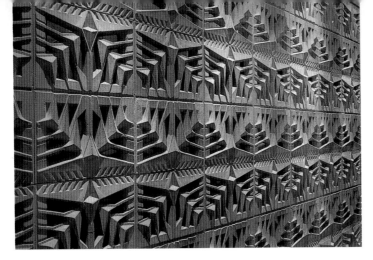

Keeping the project in the family, they turned to their architect brother, Albert, who had once apprenticed to Wright. Albert prepared sketches and preliminary studies in 1927, but then decided to contact Wright in January of 1928 about using his textile block system of construction. In severe financial straits with no commissions at the time, Wright telegraphed back an enthusiastic reply offering to come to the site to help. Within a matter of days, he arrived by train from his snowbound Wisconsin estate, anxious to be back at work, even without top billing. "I was to remain incognito and behind the scenes, glad to do so," he said.

The lowly concrete block may have seemed an unusual choice for a luxury resort hotel. But McArthur was familiar with Wright's magnificent treatment of this "gutter rat" of architecture in the classic California houses of the 1920s—Millard, Freeman, Ennis, and Storer. There Wright employed a method of construction in which delicately patterned concrete blocks were "knit" together with steel rods to form walls of "textile block." Perforated, patterned, and plain they came together in amazing combinations to create a richly textured, unified composition.

At the Arizona Biltmore, a corps of expert workmen labored around the clock to cast and set in place the 250,000 blocks needed to form the walls of

the hotel and fifteen guest cottages. Within six months, the building took shape on a remote, six-hundred-acre stretch of desert wilderness at the foot of Squaw Peak. In February 1929, the hotel opened to great fanfare and was immediately crowned the "Jewel of the Desert."

But Wright was not altogether pleased with the design or his position as behind-the-scenes consultant. Indeed, this role made it impossible for him to prevent the addition of a fourth floor, which he felt ruined the proportions, or to maintain the integrity of the block system. In the California houses, the blocks were knit together structurally to form the walls. In the Biltmore, they were reduced to a decorative veneer. Only the Wright-designed cottages situated at the rear of the hotel used the block system as intended. Events did not turn out well for the McArthur brothers either. Construction costs far

exceeded the original projections, and they had to bring in additional investors. By the time the hotel opened for a second season, one month after the stock market crash in 1929, chewing gum magnate William Wrigley emerged as the hotel's new owner.

Today one enters the Biltmore estate along a wide, palm-lined boulevard. The once remote site is now completely engulfed within the city of Phoenix. Approached from the east, the hotel presents an imposing image. Elaborate and theatrical, it stretches out 345 feet north to south upon velvety green lawns, looking more like an exotic Aztec fortress than a resort hotel. It is clear that Wright's textile block concept translates well from the small scale of a private residence to the larger proportions of a public building.

Passing through a low-ceilinged portico and entrance foyer, one emerges into the grand two-hundred-foot-long lobby. Here the true drama of the

FAR LEFT Under a vaulted ceiling of gold leaf, the two-hundred-foot-long lobby spreads out in dramatic fashion, skirted by intimate seating alcoves and illuminated by lighted glass cubes. Though it seems a luxury, the gold leaf is quite economical since it needs little maintenance.

LEFT Standing columns of faceted and plain concrete blocks inset with illuminated blocks of glass rise from a shimmering pool like an oasis in the desert to greet visitors upon their entrance to the Arizona Biltmore.

RIGHT Wright pulled out his T-square, triangle, and compass to abstract the shapes of the desert in this colorful stained glass mural, *Sahuaro Forms and Cactus Flowers,* which stands near the hotel lobby. The mural, based on a design Wright proposed for a *Liberty* magazine cover in 1927, was added by Taliesin Architects in 1973 after a six-alarm fire severely damaged the hotel, requiring an extensive renovation.

Arizona Biltmore unfolds. Magnificent in detail, this cool and comforting space confirms Wright's touch. Concrete piers covered in patterned blocks flank either side of the long, narrow room. Pairs of lighted glass blocks are scattered above like stars in a night-time sky. There appear to be no walls. Instead, the lobby spills out naturally right and left into sunlit seating coves and outdoor patios. Overhead, corbeled beams support a second-floor balcony that completely encircles the room.

At the west end of the lobby, a series of wide, shallow steps leads to the Gold Room, a spacious dining and banquet hall with radiant stained glass windows in bright green, orange, and yellow. At the opposite end of the lobby, another dining space, originally a breakfast room, is more intimate in scale. A ten-sided ballroom branches off from the main entrance. With its gold leaf ceiling, spokelike beams, and projecting bay windows, this is the room most often cited as bearing the Wright imprint. Guest rooms and several small public spaces occupy the second, third, and fourth floors. In the rear is a large octagonal patio bordered by wings of more guest rooms and a cluster of resort cottages. Other wings containing guest rooms and public spaces, some designed by Wright's successor firm, Taliesin Architects, have been added over the years.

Ever since its earliest halcyon days, the hotel has been a playground for the rich and famous. According to hotel lore, Clark Gable lost his wedding ring on the golf course, Harpo Marx and his new bride scandalized and charmed other guests by holding hands and skipping through the formal dining room, Edna Ferber wrote several novels there, and Irving Berlin supposedly composed "White Christmas" while staying at the desert resort.

A complex array of beams, Cherokee red trusses, and sheets of clear glass and plastic form the angular spaces of the Taliesin West garden room. Like the drafting studio, the garden room was originally topped by canvas, which Wright replaced in later years with various man-made materials. Wright enjoyed the luminous quality of the light as it filtered through the translucent covering. Canted square hassocks and the low plywood chairs Wright created for Taliesin West are scattered throughout the room. A wooden floor lamp with a folded plastic shade, a reproduction of an original Wright design, illuminates one corner.

TALIESIN WEST
1937-59 SCOTTSDALE, ARIZONA

IN A PARCHED LANDSCAPE of epic beauty, where giant saguaros stand sentinel in the shadow of ancient mountains, a winding road ascends gradually toward Taliesin West. Colorful rocks are strewn across the desert floor, and strange, thorny plants cluster in sparse, dusty arrangements. Before long, a rhythm of beams and stone emerges from the mystic desert vegetation. The forms are unfamiliar and do not suggest a residence. But this is no ordinary house, and no ordinary person lived here. This was the desert retreat of Frank Lloyd Wright, the place he built for himself. Here he was his own client, able to indulge his every whim to create the perfect desert home.

Wright got his first glimpse of the Arizona desert in 1928 when he traveled from his Wisconsin home, the original Taliesin, to work on the design of the Arizona Biltmore. He was smitten by what he saw—the "intoxicating air, sweeping mountain vistas, and astonishing cactus plant life"—and a few years later began exploring the area as a possible site for a second home, an escape from the long and bitter winters at his Wisconsin estate. Accompanied by members of his newly formed Taliesin Fellowship, Wright camped in the desert, traveling "to and fro like the 'possessed' from one beautiful place to another" in search of the perfect site. Finally, in late 1937, they found it—several hundred acres of rugged desert at the foothills of the McDowell Mountains.

FAR LEFT Low and sweeping, the buildings of Taliesin West spread out horizontally across the desert floor, angled on a west-southwest axis. From humble materials—canvas, redwood, desert stone, and concrete—Wright wove a rich and complex tapestry that blended harmoniously with the native vegetation and landscape. Golden brittlebush blooms in glorious profusion toward the south.

LEFT The original dining room, now offices for Taliesin Architects, runs perpendicular to the drafting studio, beneath cantilevered redwood beams. A communal kitchen and a newer, glassed-in dining room is behind it.

BELOW A series of riblike trusses supports the roof of Wright's private office. Angular and sharp, the building echoes the spiny textures of the native desert flora. A gold-and-white checkerboard shade protects the interior from the direct sun.

Unlike the softly rounded, lush green hills Wright had left behind in Wisconsin, this landscape was open, spare, and sharply sculptural. It called for a new type of building, and Wright rose to the challenge. With the desert providing both inspiration and building materials, he devised an ingenious and inexpensive method of construction using large sturdy boulders that could be plucked from the site for free. The colorful rocks were carefully placed in low wooden forms, then a thin mixture of cement was poured around them. The next day, the form was stripped and the process began again. Not only were most of the materials free, but so was the labor, supplied by Wright's willing and eager young band of apprentices. The finished product—a rich mosaic of purple, rust, orange and tan—echoed the texture, the color, and the very form of the sunburned terrain. Wright called it "desert rubblestone" and used it everywhere—from walls to ceilings, parapets to piers.

He modeled the roof system on Ocatilla, a transitory enclave of canvas-topped wooden cabins he

ABOVE Like a lantern on the desert, the drafting studio glows from within, its angular forms reflected in the thoughtfully placed triangular pool. The pool provided easy access to water in the early days when Taliesin West was miles from civilization and a fire station.

FAR RIGHT Wright loved films, which were shown weekly in the Cabaret Theater, a forty-foot-square masonry block open on the north by horizontal wooden shutters. Low concrete benches, upholstered in red, terminate in triangular built-in lights. Additional seating and folding tables make this a suitable spot for premovie dinners. A small serving kitchen is located behind the movie screen.

built in the desert south of Chandler, Arizona, in 1929. More sophisticated than Ocatilla or Ocatillo (Wright's various misspellings of the desert plant ocotillo), the Taliesin West roof was formed by a network of slanting redwood trusses set on edge above the masonry walls. Between each truss, Wright inserted panels of stout white canvas to serve as a tentlike protection. There were no glass windows and few real doors; instead, canvas flaps opened on a series of ropes and pulleys, leaving the structure open to the breezes and whims of passing wildlife. Wright said the light coming through the canvas was so agreeable that he felt oppressed at the thought of the solid-roofed midwestern homes.

During construction, the apprentice workforce camped in tents on the site, while Wright, his wife, Olgivanna, and their young daughter, Iovanna, occupied a set of primitive open-air sleeping boxes. Though seventy, the ever-vital Wright saw the experience as a great adventure, one that would sweep "the spirit clean of stagnate ways." Like a desert Daniel Boone, he was conquering new frontiers. It took several winters to complete the structure, though Wright never regarded it as finished. As he did his Wisconsin home, Wright viewed Taliesin West as a laboratory for trying out new ideas as they came to him, tearing down walls and starting again. Every so often a completely new structure would be added until the "camp," as it is still called today, grew to include offices, workshops, a drafting studio, storerooms, apprentice quarters, dining areas, guest rooms, and three theaters.

Though Taliesin West is composed of many distinct structures built over twenty years, each is so skillfully integrated with the others and the desert that the complex appears to have grown as one from its rocky site. From every angle, the buildings resonate with the patterns and the texture of the desert: walls are slanted slightly inward to mimic the slope of the mountains; the staccato redwood beams resemble the barbs of the local vegetation; and the undulating

roofline echoes the jagged silhouette of the mountain behind. When Taliesin West was nearly complete, Wright announced that it "belonged to the desert as if it had stood there for centuries."

The complex is entered from the west where a low stone wall marks the delineation between Wright's desert compound and the natural world. So beautifully composed is the native vegetation outside

LEFT TOP Wright's symbol for the Taliesin Fellowship is shaped in red metal and placed along a desert rubblestone pillar as a greeting for visitors. Adapted from a Native American petroglyph found on the site, the symbol also graced Wright's letterhead in the 1950s.

LEFT Perfectly at home in its surroundings, Taliesin West drinks in the warm desert sun. Massive desert boulders in shades of burnt umber form the canted walls of Wright's desert home.

ABOVE Wright liked the look of water in the landscape even in the desert, and placed several pools and fountains throughout the camp, including this angular one between the Kiva and the garden room wing. Beyond the low parapet are apartments for members of the Taliesin Fellowship. The tall masonry tower once held a water tank.

the wall, one could imagine Wright's hand in arranging it. The first visible structure on the site is a compact, angular stone building, topped by a canted series of redwood beams. Positioned partially underground at a forty-five-degree angle, this was Wright's office. In the quiet confines of this private domain, Wright met with clients and dictated correspondence.

Extending from the office to the north is the Cabaret Theater, a bunkerlike space with a fireplace at one end and a screen for movies at the other. Wright was fond of movies and counted several Hollywood stars among his friends, including the actor Charles Laughton, who sometimes held readings of the Bible there. Farther to the north, Wright built a concert hall for his daughter, Iovanna, who was a musician and choreographer. Unlike the dark, rather austere Cabaret, the Pavilion is an airy, bright structure with translucent ceilings and a vibrant red color scheme. Rebuilt after a fire in 1962, it was the site of many Taliesin Fellowship dance performances, choreographed by Iovanna with music composed by Wright's wife, Olgivanna.

Across a garden courtyard, a trellis-covered walkway leads to the drafting studio, the heart of the complex. Ninety-six feet long and thirty feet wide, the space holds drafting tables for about twenty-five architects. Along the south wall, a long bank of low windows looks toward the desert and the cities of Scottsdale and Phoenix below. On the north, a series of taller windows and solid French doors opens onto a vista of the majestic McDowell Mountains. Once protected by a canvas roof, the room is now topped by translucent plastic panels. After years of struggling with the deteriorating effects of the harsh sun, Wright replaced all

of the canvas roofs in the camp with more durable man-made materials. A communal kitchen and glass-enclosed dining room are situated east of the studio.

A wide breezeway with an outdoor fireplace marks the transition between the studio complex and the living quarters. The garden room, designed and continually changed by Wright, was considered the Taliesin Fellowship living room, the frequent site of Sunday evening parties and other social occasions. At fifty-six feet long and thirty-four feet wide, the room is as large as an average family home. The original movie theater, named the Kiva by Wright, is located on the eastern edge of the camp. This rectangular stone fortress, with only two small windows and a hefty wooden door, was one of the earliest structures to be built. Its flat stone roof often served as a gathering area for afternoon tea, a daily ritual. Today the Kiva is used as a conference room for Taliesin Architects. To the north of the Kiva is a series of apprentice apartments, built in the years before World War II. Beyond this complex is the site of the original Sun Trap, a primitive shelter occupied by the Wrights between 1938 and 1941. In 1948 a new structure, the Sun Cottage, was built on its foundation.

The construction of Taliesin West set Wright and the Taliesin Fellowship on an exhilarating new phase. Except for a short period during World War II, the entire group would migrate each spring and fall between the original Taliesin in Wisconsin and Taliesin West, a tradition that continues to this day with members of the Taliesin Fellowship. It also marked the rebirth of Wright's career, unleashing a burst of creative energy and public acclaim that continued throughout the next two decades.

Tall and angular like the region's indigenous trees, the tepeelike roof of the Friedman residence shelters the combined living and dining space below. Wright positioned a narrow band of clerestory windows where the tallest peak engages the gently flared lower roof, forcing daylight into the center of the house.

FRIEDMAN RESIDENCE

1945 PECOS, NEW MEXICO

EARLY IN HIS CAREER, Wright looked to the landscape to create ground-hugging horizontal structures in league with the flat midwestern prairies. As his architecture matured, he continued to learn from nature, searching its forms for fresh inspiration. In developing his design for the Friedman house, Wright looked to the local New Mexican piñon pines to create a peaked-roofed house he called the "Fir Tree." Harking back to an unbuilt project of 1923, the Friedman residence is the first implementation of the tepeelike roof he envisioned for a series of cabins near Lake Tahoe, California.

Exposed rafters made of rough-hewn pine and walls of indigenous stone make the Friedman house a natural analogue to the rugged New Mexican landscape. Set into a sloping site, with views of the Sangre de Cristo Mountains, the house expands vigorously northwest to southeast across the stony landscape. Since it was not initially intended for year-round occupancy, Wright provided no central heat. Instead, all rooms—bedrooms, den, living and dining spaces—are equipped with their own fireplaces to provide warmth on cool evenings.

Wright based the floor plan of this two-thousand-square-foot residence on a diamond-shaped grid. The unit is scored into the red concrete floors and found elsewhere in furnishings and masonry piers. The peaked

THE FIR-TREE FOR ARNOLD FRIEDMAN, PECOS, NEW MEX

roof, composed of shake-covered triangles, also rein-forces the theme. Narrow and angular like the region's native pines, it is poised on a band of clerestory windows that bring natural light into the living and dining space below. In this combined space, Wright placed a generous fireplace on the south wall opposing a light and transparent wall of glass doors on the north. These doors open onto a prow-shaped terrace protected by a low, desert masonry wall. The bedrooms branch off the living room in two connected wings that wrap around a central, grassy court.

John de Koven Hill, an apprentice to Wright, designed the interior furnishings, which include an innovative floor covering composed of diamond-shaped cowhide skins lashed together with leather thongs. Hill also designed the rough-cut pine furni-ture covered in a pale yellow upholstery, and a set of heavy pine deck chairs for the Friedman's terrace.

Romantic and rustic, charming yet noble, this house truly expresses Wright's concept of indigenous architecture. Completely discrediting the cold, aus-tere style of the Internationalists, who Wright felt had no sense of place, this house reflects the moun-tains, the trees, and the rock outcroppings of its beautiful New Mexico site.

Wright believed that houses should be as different as their owners, expressing the individual character and needs of the inhabitants. For Chauncey Griggs, an art collector and lumber company owner, he created a vast gallery for the display of artwork with soaring lumber trusses providing drama overhead. Doors on the right lead to bedrooms. On the left, glass doors open to a stone-paved terrace. At the far end is the master bedroom.

GRIGGS RESIDENCE
1946 TACOMA, WASHINGTON

DEEP WITHIN A FORESTED GLEN, where toppled logs are covered in dense thickets of ivy and the air is ripe with the sweet scent of pine, a footbridge crosses Chambers Creek onto an open meadow and the commanding presence of the Chauncey Griggs residence. Set well back from the water's edge, this "Northern Timber House," as Wright called it, embodies the notion of a house in tune with its native surroundings, in this case the Pacific Northwest.

To achieve the character he felt appropriate for the region, Wright selected a wood-frame construction of rough-sawn cedar boards. Rather than place the boards vertically or horizontally, Wright arranged them diagonally to follow the slant of the shed roof. Covered in cedar shakes, the graceful roof tilts nearly to the ground at the back edge of the house, but sweeps rapidly to two stories at the front. The rustic simplicity of natural materials complements the building's elegant form.

Inside, the character of the great Northwest again comes into play in spaces so overwhelming in scale that one still feels outdoors. This is particularly true in the two-story open gallery with its soaring composition of timber trusses overhead and the thirty-foot-long wall of glass to the south. Such a lofty scale is unusual for a Usonian house—Wright's concept of affordable housing for the middle class—particularly in the gallery, typically

a simple narrow hallway leading to the bedrooms. But Chauncey and Johanna Griggs wanted a room large enough to hold exhibitions of their art collection; thus Wright expanded the space to fourteen by thirty-five feet, with six tall glass doors on the south to drink in the summer sun. When the doors are open, the room merges with a stone-paved terrace, enlarging the space even more as it connects to the outdoors.

The gallery forms the long leg of the L-shaped plan, with four small bedrooms opening onto the space. It terminates in a "sanctum," as Wright labeled the drawings, a fourteen-by-twenty-foot room that could serve equally well as a private study or large master bedroom. The other leg of the L holds the kitchen, the living room, and a "lounge"

for holding chamber music concerts. A dining area was cleverly bumped out from the inside corner of the L, with windows to the south. A masonry core of concrete block forms the walls of the kitchen and encloses two fireplaces, one facing the lounge, the other facing the dining area.

LEFT TOP The roof reaches low at the back of the house over the bedrooms but rises up to a great height in the front, sweeping out over walls to create a deep, protective overhang. Thick cedar boards are situated diagonally to echo the slope of the shed roof.

LEFT BOTTOM Chambers Creek, viewed from the carport, flows along the southern and eastern edges of the heavily wooded Griggs' property.

RIGHT Because Wright felt that southern light was the most pleasing, he generally conceived of the south side of a house as the "living side." These corner windows in the dining room face directly south. The whimsical dining set was added by the current owner.

The house is placed on a thirty-sixty-degree diagonal facing south, Wright's preferred positioning. Rarely, if he had a choice, did Wright place a house on a direct north-south axis, since this inevitably resulted in the house having a dark side. Angled to the south, each room has sunlight sometime during the day. Wright designed no furniture or fixtures for the house, so the Griggs were left to their own devices to furnish the three-thousand-square-foot space. The floors are of poured concrete, but are not Cherokee red, as was the general custom. Instead, they are of a highly polished greenish brown, perhaps in keeping with the woodsy feel. The grid scored into the concrete is an uncommon one for Wright—a seven-foot square.

Wright originally planned to build the house of split-log construction and sandstone masonry. Griggs, in the timber business himself, was not keen on a log house, preferring something he considered more elegant. Though the house was designed in 1946, construction did not begin until nearly seven years later. By then estimates for the stonework were so prohibitive that Griggs suggested concrete block masonry to Wright after visiting the Wright-designed Brandes residence nearby. Wright approved of the change, but did not oversee the alteration. That was left to a local architect, Alan Liddle, who also supervised the construction.

FAR LEFT Griggs and his wife, Johanna, both avid music fans, requested a room large enough for chamber concerts. The "lounge," as Wright labeled the space, holds a grand piano and also serves as a living room. Floor-to-ceiling windows harness as much daylight as possible in the rainy northwestern climate.

LEFT A concrete-block fireplace positioned near the entryway in the living room provides welcoming warmth. The kitchen, located behind the fireplace mass, shares the masonry wall. Wright originally planned stone for all of the masonry, but it was changed to concrete block because of soaring postwar construction costs.

CARLSON RESIDENCE

1950   PHOENIX, ARIZONA

Wright gave the Raymond Carlson house
his seal of approval by pulling out a pen
and writing "Hurrah Ray FLLW" right on
the house.

Wright designed the house on a grid system of four-foot squares, using modular panels of gray transite between the redwood posts. The entrance is sheltered beneath the lower cantilevered plane, between the tower and the living room wing.

MANY WRIGHT-DESIGNED HOMES bear his red signature tile as a mark of authenticity, but the Raymond Carlson house is the only one Wright signed with his own hand. On his way to the Phoenix airport one day from his Taliesin West home, Wright asked his driver to stop at the Carlson house. No one was home, so Wright took out a pen and wrote "Hurrah Ray FLLW" directly on the wall next to the front door. When Carlson returned, he immediately recognized the signature and wisely shellacked it for posterity.

As was often the case with Wright's clients, Carlson was also a friend. The two became acquainted in 1940 when Carlson, editor of *Arizona Highways* magazine, asked Wright to prepare an article for the fall issue. Over the years Carlson featured Wright several times in the magazine and often attended social occasions at Taliesin West with his wife, Helen. The Carlsons had a limited budget, but Wright told them that if they found a site, he would design them a house.

In the evening, the Carlson house glitters radiantly, illuminated by built-in fixtures embedded in the ceiling and the exterior soffits. The one-story living room spreads out horizontally from the tower, its walls of glass facing north.

To keep costs down for his friends, Wright chose inexpensive building materials and a simple modular plan. Redwood four-by-fours, notched and doweled, were used for support, with panels of gray transite (a combination of asbestos and cement) in between. Challenged by a site that was less than ideal —a pie-shaped corner lot in a Phoenix tract development—Wright angled the house diagonally, southwest to northeast, with the narrow end facing the street corner. To ensure privacy, he placed the bedrooms and kitchen in a distinctive two-and-one-half-story tower, uniquely positioning floors at half levels away from the neighbors' direct gaze.

Long, low, and sleek, the house has been likened to a classic wood-framed yacht. Sweeping and intricate horizontal lines ground the house to the earth, while the tower provides a distinct vertical contrast. Capped by a sharp horizontal plane that

appears to float on air, the tower's imposing shaft of gray transite is counterpointed by a complex grid of vivid blue struts. The tower itself, which terminates at ground level on a band of recessed windows, also appears to levitate. Though only about eleven hundred square feet, the house seems much larger, primarily due to Wright's extensive, yet judicious, use of glass.

One enters the house from the north and immediately encounters the masonry core. Rising up twenty-five feet, it links the vertical tower with the horizontal living room wing. Three fireplaces are stacked within its concrete block walls: one in the dining area below grade, one in the living room at ground level, and one on the rooftop terrace. The living room wing spreads out to the west with built-in

FROM LEFT TO RIGHT Inside the house, the redwood struts are left natural, but where they intersect exterior walls, they are painted a brilliant blue enamel to intensify the building's complex geometries. This end of the house originally held a carport, later remodeled into a glass-enclosed study.

The tower, which holds the kitchen and dining room below grade, two bedrooms and a bath on the second floor, and a penthouse study at the top, appears to float on a recessed layer of windows that look directly onto a ground-level garden. Except for a band of clerestories at the top, few other windows were provided on the west side of the house to maintain privacy and keep the interior cool.

Twelve windows, bordered in a grid of blue struts, shine daylight on the narrow staircase that rises through the tower.

seating arranged along the south and west walls to free up valuable floor space. High clerestory windows above the seating area minimize the direct rays of bright desert sun, yet allow daylight to bounce off cantilevered decking into the room. On the cooler, northern side, Wright placed a bank of floor-to-ceiling windows and French doors that open onto a terrace of scored red concrete.

The tower rooms are accessed by a narrow staircase, just twenty-two inches wide. Up a half level is the master bedroom and guest room. Faced in Douglas fir plywood, both are quite compact and snug, yet well supplied with built-in closets and dressers. Directly above the bedrooms is Carlson's penthouse study. Perched in this lofty sanctuary, he could work quietly at his built-in desk or step just

outside to the rooftop terrace. The lowest level of the tower holds the dining area and kitchen, where Wright's clever half-floor positioning has the most impact and charm. With the space set six feet below grade, diners and the cook look directly outside through a band of ribbon windows into a recessed planting area.

The Carlsons did much of the construction themselves, the kind of commitment that often summoned the most personal attention from Wright. Wright was apparently so pleased with the result that he returned his architect's commission. "It is so finely built," he wrote, "I am giving half my fee to the builder as a reward of merit; the rest of the fee goes to Raymond himself to help furnish his aristocratic little gem of a house."

Unlike a traditional home with a definite front facade, this twisted coil of concrete block seems to have no front or back. One must move around the house to make sense of it; yet with every step, the house changes in mood and appearance. The entrance is hidden beneath the flared galvanized metal roof on the second level.

DAVID WRIGHT RESIDENCE

1950 PHOENIX, ARIZONA

FRANK LLOYD WRIGHT designed homes for two of his sons, one for Llewellyn in Bethesda, Maryland, another for David in Phoenix. Both were based on unusual geometric forms, with circles and arcs replacing more familiar straight lines. Llewellyn's sleek ellipse of wood and David's swirling coil of concrete block both artfully challenge the concept of what a house should look like, a notion they must have anticipated when they asked their father for a design.

With all living spaces suspended off the ground, the David Wright residence is the realization of the elder Wright's vision of "How to Live in the Southwest," the title he gave the drawings when they were published in *House and Home* magazine in 1953. Wright believed that lifting the house off the hot desert floor would allow breezes to flow freely beneath it, cooling the spaces above. There was no need to plant grass. The treetops would be the lawn.

The house was originally conceived in wood, but Wright changed the material at his son's urging. An executive in the concrete block business, David felt compelled to prove that the common concrete block could be as beautiful as cut stone. No stranger himself to the versatile concrete block, Wright complied with his son's wishes, making the rectangular blocks conform to a radial plan by butting them tightly on the inside of the

LEFT Wright's curved in-line plan is obvious in this aerial photograph taken in 1959. A long entry ramp sweeps up from the desert floor, around a central courtyard, to the second level where the house itself begins.

ABOVE LEFT Gladys Wright's porthole window in the kitchen illuminates cabinets and counter tops that follow the curve of the wall. The same material—concrete block—inside and out adds unity to the design in this 1953 photograph.

ABOVE RIGHT Wright brought the circular theme inside the house with a round dining table, a curved ceiling, and half-moon clerestory windows. A few recessed lights appear near the ceiling, but most artificial lighting comes from the exterior flood-lights that shine through the glass walls into the house. Thus, whether day or night, light seems to come from the same source.

curve and mortaring them widely on the outside. In Wright's supple hands, the standard modular blocks became a sculpture of swirls, curls, and sweeping arcs.

Although the two-thousand-square-foot house appears from some vantage points to be a solid circle, it is actually a ramplike coil that lifts off the ground as it curves. To accomplish this feat, Wright took his classic in-line plan—where all rooms are laid

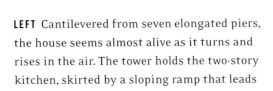

LEFT Cantilevered from seven elongated piers, the house seems almost alive as it turns and rises in the air. The tower holds the two-story kitchen, skirted by a sloping ramp that leads to a rooftop garden. A narrow, round chimney peaks out above.

RIGHT Summoning a new form for the humble concrete block, Wright gave his son a house of curves, circles, and arcs. Shadows formed by the house offer protection to shade-loving plants and shrubs below.

end to end—and twisted it until the head was poised over the tail. The advantages are many: a short corridor, pie-shaped rooms that open out to magnificent views, and a sense of comfort from organic, curving forms that seem more natural and friendly to the human experience than the straight line. Seven elongated piers of reinforced concrete block support the structure as it turns and sweeps upward. The roof is of galvanized metal.

The journey through the house begins at a ground-level ramp that rises gently around a central courtyard. With each forward step, stunning vistas dissolve and form. Directly to the north is Camelback Mountain, to the south the Papago Park buttes. About ten feet off the ground and a third of the way around the circle, one enters the house, a dazzling display of curves and arcs. Half-circle windows, a ceiling of curved mahogany boards, a round fireplace, and a carpet of colorful interlocking arcs draw the eye around the living room, the principal space in the house.

Behind the living room fireplace, Wright placed the kitchen in its own compact tower, where everything is within easy reach. Though he did not plan an eye-level window (he preferred skylights or high clerestories in the kitchen), his daughter-in-law insisted. Wright gave her a large, round, customdesigned porthole. Branching off from the living room toward the east, two pie-shaped bedrooms open onto a curved corridor, illuminated by a band of casement windows set above built-in bookshelves. Wright concluded his composition with a dramatic flourish—a semicircular master bedroom daringly poised over the foot of the entry ramp, with 180-degree mountain views and a cozy curved fireplace.

ADELMAN RESIDENCE

1951 PHOENIX, ARIZONA

LOCATED IN THE LOOMING SHADOW of Squaw Peak, adjacent to the Arizona Biltmore estate, the Benjamin Adelman house is regarded as the first "Usonian Automatic," a building system Wright developed for veterans of World War II. Based on a concept similar to the California textile block houses, the Usonian Automatics were built of specially crafted concrete blocks that could be assembled in an infinite number of ways, much like children's building blocks. Though these blocks were not as ornamental as the delicately patterned textile blocks, the method of construction was the same: Hollow, half blocks of concrete, usually one by two feet, were cast with a half-circle groove at the edge. When two blocks were placed together, the grooves joined to form a shaft into which thin steel rods were threaded horizontally and vertically, tying the blocks together to form a wall.

Wright believed these houses could easily be self-built, eliminating the expense of skilled union labor, particularly for the financially pressed GIs. Benjamin Adelman, however, was not a GI, nor did he plan to build the house himself. Instead, his son, Albert, who handled the project for his father, engaged two of Wright's former apprentices, Charles Montooth and Arthur Pieper, to take charge of construction in late 1952. Wright assisted the Adelmans in securing an acre of desert near the Biltmore from his client Jorgine Boomer, whose own Wright-designed cottage is located next door. Over the years, Wright designed half a dozen projects for the

LEFT Flat roofs and dominant horizontal lines give the Adelman residence, viewed from the east, a graceful, earth-hugging silhouette. A large master bedroom wing and garage, on the right, were added in the 1980s, nearly doubling the size of the original.

RIGHT Metal cames painted Wright's favorite Cherokee red divide the windows of the living room into two-foot squares that enliven the exterior. The main entry, which was moved from the south to the east side of the house, is located on the right.

ABOVE The first Usonian Automatic designed for a client, the Adelman residence is composed of specially cast concrete blocks, some coffered as in the living room ceiling, some perforated to hold glass, and some plain. The name *Usonian* referred to the United States; the word *automatic* suggested an easy, do-it-yourself concept. The modular plywood furniture was copied from a Wright design. The vinyl flooring is marked with a grid to match Wright's two-foot unit.

Wright eliminated unnecessary walls that confined movement, allowing the dining room and living room to flow as one uninterrupted space. Texture and detailing of the walls is the same inside and outside, creating a sense of organic unity.

BELOW A stunning mural of abstract geometric shapes hangs above the living room fireplace. Designed by artist and Wright assistant Eugene Masselink, it adds a colorful contrast to the gray concrete blocks. Simple built-in shelves and cabinets conserve space. The perforated screen, added in the 1980s, opens into the kitchen.

In the 1980s, the open terrace leading from the main house to the guest wing in the back was enclosed with glass and turned into a hallway. Lighting fixtures are embedded in the coffered ceiling. The guest wing, which held a maid's room, guest room, and sitting area, was converted into two bedrooms and two baths.

Adelman family, including a laundry plant, three homes for Benjamin, and two for Albert. Of these works, only this house for Benjamin and another for Albert near Milwaukee, Wisconsin, were built. Though the Benjamin Adelman residence is considered the first Usonian Automatic designed by Wright, it was not the first one built. That distinction belongs to the prototype Pieper house, built in Phoenix in early 1952.

In consideration of the family's need for a winter home that could accommodate their many visitors from the Midwest, Wright designed two small buildings—a guest house and a main residence—connected by a covered walkway. The seven-hundred-square-foot main quarters, square in plan, contained the master bedroom, bath, living and dining space, and kitchen. The long and narrow five-hundred-square-foot guest house, running north to south behind the main house, included two tiny bedrooms, two baths, and a sitting room with a fireplace. Based on a two-foot-square module, the house went through many revisions before Wright settled on this plan.

Benjamin Adelman died in 1959, and the house was sold soon thereafter. Under a succession of owners, the house deteriorated so badly that by the late 1980s major structural repair was needed just to save it. In correcting years of damage, the new owners took many liberties with the original design: The severely damaged block, seemingly beyond repair, was sprayed with a grayish green textured stucco, the entrance was moved from the south wall to the east, the open terrace between the two wings was enclosed, the kitchen was enlarged, the red concrete floor was covered with red vinyl painted with dark lines to mirror the original scoring, and most significantly, a large master bedroom wing and two-car garage were added to the north. The many changes significantly alter Wright's original concept for a "Desert Cottage," as he labeled the drawings, and one wonders how he might have perceived such a transformation. Nevertheless, the house still stands as an important record of Wright's first Usonian Automatic, a building he proudly published in his most famous treatise on American residential design, *The Natural House,* in 1954.

LEFT "I'm a log cabin man," Quintin Blair told Wright when the architect offered to design the couple a house, "so you talk to my girl." With Ruth's input, they got something considerably more sophisticated: a stunning residence of glass, sandstone, and wood.

RIGHT The Blair residence reflects off the glassy pond like a faceted jewel. Years of arduous landscaping and the damming of a creek turned the normally dusty Wyoming terrain into a lush oasis. The light standard and the planter on the left were designed by Bruce Goff.

BLAIR RESIDENCE
1952 CODY, WYOMING

FRANK LLOYD WRIGHT, at eighty-five, stood in his driveway at Taliesin West, cape flowing and porkpie hat perched on his head, when Quintin and Ruth Blair drove up to his Arizona home uninvited. Although he had never met the young Wyoming couple, Wright immediately walked over to the car and insisted that they stay awhile. After lunch and an impromptu tour, Wright impulsively offered to design a house for them. "Hell, I can't afford you" was Quintin Blair's honest and blunt reply. "Don't worry," Wright calmly assured him. "I won't cost you a dime more than anyone else."

After returning home from their Arizona vacation and unexpected encounter with Wright, the Blairs purchased a sixty-acre tract of gently rolling Wyoming countryside a few miles outside of Cody. The bleak site had a narrow stream but almost no vegetation. They sent Wright an aerial photograph and immediately began to plant trees. Today, the elegant house Wright designed for them is hidden from the road by a dense thicket of Russian olive, cottonwood, blue spruce, and honey locust trees. A large, trout-filled pond, the result of damming the stream, offers refreshing views to the east from the living room, dining room, and kitchen.

RIGHT Walls of mitered glass enclose three sides of the living room, flooding the interior with natural light. Where glass meets glass, the barrier between interior and exterior blurs, and the entire room seems to merge with the eastern sky. The pitched, butterfly roof is supported by steel I beams anchored into the masonry core at the center of the house. The ceiling is sheathed in Philippine mahogany.

FAR RIGHT Glass corners allow one to glimpse straight through the house. Although the house ultimately cost far more than Wright projected, the Blairs were never sorry they took him up on the offer.

Built of Philippine mahogany, glass, and a colorful mosaic of red and gold sandstone quarried in nearby Cowley, Wyoming, the Blair house is rectangular in plan with one intriguing variation. Wright rotated the lower masonry walls in the living room wing forty-five degrees, but continued the roof and glass walls in-line with the bedroom wing. At the point where the walls rotate, the roof rises rapidly from seven and one-half feet to fifteen feet and then sweeps out over mitered glass walls.

This seven-hundred-square-foot space—originally a combined living room, kitchen, and dining area—is the nucleus of the house and the place where

Wright lavished his greatest care. The room's golden-hued mahogany ceiling, intimate built-in seating areas, angular sandstone fireplace, and expansive walls of glass evoke elegance and graciousness. Wright even designed a special sandstone niche for the Blairs' grand piano. When Ruth Blair told Wright they didn't own a grand piano, he replied simply, "You go buy one."

The two original bedrooms in this one-story house, though quite small, are efficient and convenient. Everything is built in—bookcases, dressers, even special racks for shoes. Like a fine cabinet, the detailing is seamless and meticulous, from the lapped board mahogany ceilings to the board-and-batten mahogany walls. Privacy is absolute, as the rooms' only windows are high clerestories covered with wooden cutout shapes (Wright called them perforated boards) that filter soft light into the spaces. Just outside the bedrooms to the south, Wright designed a twenty-eight-foot-long sleeping porch with French doors that opened onto a terrace and views of the pond.

As with so many of Wright's clients who were unable to hire contractors willing to deal with the complexities of his designs, Quintin Blair had to supervise the construction himself. When problems arose, he would call Wright at Taliesin. "And what's wrong now, Brother Blair?" Wright would boom into the phone. Blair would explain that his workmen couldn't miter glass. "Well, have they ever tried it?" Wright would ask. "No," Blair replied. "Then you tell them to try, and if they can't do it, I'll come there myself!"

The Blairs have made several changes to the house since they finished it in 1954, more than doubling its original fifteen hundred square feet. After Wright's death, Ruth Blair contacted her teacher and friend, architect Bruce Goff, about designing an addition. It was Goff who first introduced Ruth Blair to Wright's work. In the spirit of Wright, Goff enclosed the open sleeping porch to create a formal dining room, transformed Wright's original laundry room into a large kitchen, and added a two-car garage faced in board-and-batten Philippine mahogany on the south side. The Blairs planned a second addition by Goff, but when he died in 1982, they turned to Charles Montooth of Taliesin Architects to design a large master bedroom and connecting atrium. This was completed in 1992.

Despite the prevailing notion that Wright could be difficult, the Blairs found just the opposite to be true. "He was a nice man to work with," Quintin Blair recalls. "I would send him a big cheese every Christmas and he would always send back a poem. But I never did figure out why he called me Brother Blair."

FAR LEFT The Blairs had architect Bruce Goff enclose the open sleeping porch with glass to create a formal dining area that looks out to the pond. The deeply coffered mahogany ceiling adds depth and texture to the room. The table is an original Wright design; the ca. 1900 chairs are from a lodge in nearby Yellowstone National Park.

LEFT TOP Wright gave the grand piano its own space in the Blair residence, a triangular niche of red and gold sandstone embedded into walls of glass.

LEFT BOTTOM Opposite the glass walls, the solid masonry core juts into the living room like a prow. A supporting wall of sandstone holds built-in seating and bookshelves. The multicolor carpet was designed by John de Koven Hill.

BRANDES RESIDENCE

1952 ISSAQUAH, WASHINGTON

EXTENSIVE USE OF NATURAL LIGHT, the alternating textures of smooth-finished redwood and rough concrete block, and the pungent scent of native fir were combined by Wright to create for Ray and Mimi Brandes a house that pleased and delighted all of the senses. Broad, horizontal, and low, the Brandes residence is remarkable not only in its ground-hugging orientation to the site, but also in its response to the overcast days typical of the northwestern climate. Situated diagonally upon a natural plateau, the house takes maximum advantage of the morning and afternoon daylight with long bands of east- and west-facing windows. A freestanding clerestory in the kitchen and living area forces additional light into the farthest reaches of the home, making certain that "every room might have sunlight some time in the day," Wright said.

With nearly twenty acres to work with, Wright had ample room to stretch this nineteen-hundred-square-foot home across its richly wooded site. Set into a broad, sloping meadow, the house, workshop, and connecting carport reach 112 feet across the landscape, evoking not only a sense of the ground, but also a sense of shelter, spaciousness, and freedom, all the salient aspects of Wright's Usonian houses.

Ray Brandes was sympathetic with Wright's Usonian philosophy, particularly his efforts to bring a well-designed house within the financial reach of the average individual. After reading a number of articles about

Wright brought the Brandes House down into a "quiet relation-
ship with the ground" by emphasizing the building's horizontal
thrust. Long bands of casement windows, deep sheltering
eaves, and concrete blocks set in receding courses allow the
house to rest comfortably within its wooded setting. It is seen
here from the north.

Wright's Usonian houses, Brandes wrote a letter to
Wright in 1951 expressing his desire for a low-cost
house compatible with his family's "simple, unaffected,
servant-less" lifestyle. A builder and contractor by
profession, Brandes planned to do much of the car-
pentry himself. Wright responded favorably and by
May of 1952 submitted his design to Ray and Mimi
Brandes. With only minor changes, the design was
quickly approved, and construction began.

Wright did not have a telephone at Taliesin
West at the time. When immediate construction problems arose, Brandes found it necessary to communicate
via telegram. He once urged Wright to call him collect,
but Wright telegrammed back that calling was too difficult since the nearest phone was fifteen miles away.
Fortunately some of the complicated construction
issues were solved by Milton Stricker, a former Wright
apprentice who had relocated to the Seattle area.

Wright selected redwood, glass, and an unusual
pink-hued concrete block as the main building
materials for the one-story residence. To further
emphasize the horizontal thrust of the house, he had
the block walls battered slightly inward, creating a
pronounced horizontal shadow where each block
course receded from the next. All of this was set upon
a red concrete pad, scored with the four-foot-square
module on which Wright based his design.

The house is entered from the rear through a
series of northeast-facing French doors that lead
directly into the combination living and dining
room, "a single spacious, harmonious unit" as Wright
described the open plan he promoted in his Usonian
houses. Once inside, the exterior vista unfolds
through a wide ribbon of casement windows that look
southwest toward a stand of towering fir trees and a
broad expanse of lawn. As engineered by Wright, the

view becomes the decoration, rendering all need for further adornment unnecessary.

Within the living and dining space, Wright created several intimate zones for conversation, reading, or relaxing. A large slab of redwood plywood, which serves as the family dining table, marks the transition between dining area and kitchen. Tucked behind the masonry core, the kitchen is equipped with stainless steel countertops and built-in cabinetry. Wright designed the built-in furnishings as well as the freestanding pieces, which were handcrafted by Brandes of redwood lumber and plywood.

At the southeastern terminus of the house, Wright placed three small bedrooms in-line, providing each with a glass door opening onto a stone terrace. Although the rooms are comfortable and filled with natural light, their small size forces the occupants out into the great living space. This social engineering was planned by Wright, who felt it was entirely appropriate to encourage family members to interact rather than isolate themselves in bedrooms. As he typically did in his other Usonian designs, Wright eliminated the need for a basement or a garage, considering them costly and unnecessary. Instead, he gave Ray Brandes a large carport connected to a private workshop, outfitted with its own fireplace.

ABOVE There are no barriers between the living and dining areas, which form one large space. Simple cushion-topped stools are tucked beneath a redwood slab dining table. The kitchen is in the rear, behind the fireplace mass.

FAR LEFT Wright provided the Brandes family with two seating zones in the living area, one with comfortable freestanding chairs opening onto a view and another adjacent to the fireplace with cozy, built-in seating. A double clerestory brings natural light deep within the structure. Translucent white cubes built into the bookcases and recessed square lights in the ceiling provide additional illumination.

LEFT Wright pushed the roofline far beyond the wall to create a sense of shelter, but punctured rectangular openings in the eave to bring daylight into the living room.

RIGHT Each of the three bedrooms opens onto a red concrete mat and stone-paved terrace. The master bedroom, situated at the end, benefits from its placement with two sets of French doors that open at the corner. A third set of French doors, leading from the terrace to the living room, can be seen in the background.

FAR RIGHT A wall of French doors on the northeast opens from the dining area onto a flagstone patio. The masonry mass on the left holds the master bathroom. On the right is the kitchen, carport, and workshop.

The prow-shaped roof of the Teater residence sweeps upward toward distant mountain views, seeming to borrow momentum from the swirling Snake River below.

TEATER STUDIO AND RESIDENCE

1952 BLISS, IDAHO

SET INTO A KNOLL on a high bluff overlooking the Snake River, the studio Wright designed for artist Archie Teater looks as natural as if it had been carved from the cliff wall itself. This might be considered something of a miracle since Wright never saw the site. Such was often the case in the last and busiest decade of Wright's career. Apparently, it was no handicap for the architect, who took maximum advantage of topographical maps and photographic surveys to integrate his designs into their natural surroundings. Taming this small corner of rocky terrain, Wright placed the studio squarely within sight and sound of nature's bounties, providing Teater, a painter of landscapes, with perhaps his greatest inspiration.

Wright designed Teater's Knoll, as the studio came to be known, in response to a lofty proposition by Teater's wife, Patricia. "We want to build a spot of interest to humanity," she wrote grandly to Wright. "Our studio would draw visitors from the entire state and beyond. It would be a symbol. It would mean so much to those who never believed in anything beyond their daily grind." Though the project was small, her entreaty caught Wright's ear and he accepted the commission.

Constructed of wood, glass, and native stone, the nineteen-hundred-square-foot studio-residence is essentially one large room. Wright based the design on a five-foot parallelogram unit, using a grid of these

VIEW FROM SOUTHWEST

units to organize and unify the space. Location of walls, windows, doors, and a fireplace is determined by the grid, as is the shape of freestanding and built-in furnishings. The concrete floor is scored with it, and walls of glass are composed of individual parallelogram-shaped panes. Though the unit is pervasive, it is not monotonous. Instead, it creates a harmonious whole, assuring that everything is kept within pleasing proportions.

Because Teater was an artist, Wright faced the main exposure north, the painter's favored light, rather than his more customary southern exposure. Walls of glass sweep upward to nineteen feet at their highest point, bathing the studio in natural light. Overhead, triangular light boxes mounted to the ceiling boards provide illumination after sunset. One compact bedroom and one bath are carved out of the eastern third of the studio near the fireplace, with an efficient kitchen and a workshop tucked behind the masonry core. There is no dining room. Instead, a parallelogram-shaped dining table placed near the kitchen defines the dining space.

The views and the architecture nourished the artist and his wife for many years, and Teater's career blossomed. But when the couple moved to California, the house was virtually abandoned. Surrounded by a fence topped with barbed wire, the house slumped into disrepair. Then in 1982, a new owner set about restoring it. He enlarged the bathroom and kitchen, pushing them into the space formerly occupied by the workshop. All of the windows were replaced, the wood was refinished, structural problems were solved, and new furniture and cabinets were built to complement the angular dining table and straight-back chairs Wright created for the house.

PIEPER RESIDENCE

1952 PARADISE VALLEY, ARIZONA

THE ARTHUR PIEPER RESIDENCE represents an important milestone in the history of Wright's Usonian Automatics. Designed for an apprentice, it was the testing ground for a standardized construction technique Wright devised to address the housing shortage following World War II. Though not the first Usonian Automatic designed, it was the first one built. A modest endeavor at just fourteen hundred square feet, it played a gallant role in setting the stage for more elegant and elaborate models that would follow. Unfortunately, its small size, exquisite site and unusual building system eventually conspired against it. Constructed on what is now some of the last open desert in metropolitan Phoenix, the house was purchased for its site and incorporated into a new addition. At forty-five hundred square feet, the so-called addition is three times the size of the original.

Arthur Pieper was an industrious young man with the ambitious goal of starting his own construction company when he joined forces with another Wright apprentice, Charles Montooth, to form Horizon Builders. Though Wright was often scornful of apprentices that left the fold, he encouraged their efforts and persuaded several of his clients to hire them. Their first customer was Benjamin Adelman, for whom Wright designed the original Usonian Automatic in nearby Phoenix. To give his young protégés some critical hands-on experience,

Years of neglect and a revolutionary building method, which some may have thought too odd or too bold, conspired against the Pieper residence. It is now just a wing of a larger structure. Looking toward the rear of the house, the taller section, on the right, originally held the combined living and dining room and the kitchen; the main entrance was at the center beneath the lower roof; and two bedrooms stretched toward the left.

Some of the three-inch-thick blocks were open at the center to hold glass inserts. Others were plain or corner blocks. All were knit together with slender rods of steel and grouting. These glass walls on the east end of the house enclose the living room.

Wright designed a house for Pieper and his wife, Bodil, that would serve as a prototype. (Pieper is of some import in Wright's personal history: his second wife was Wright's daughter, Iovanna.)

For this early, simple design, Wright specified only three types of concrete blocks: a standard wall block, a corner block, and a fascia block. Later versions would use as many as ten or twelve different block types. About half of the blocks were made on-site; the rest were cast in nearby Mesa and brought to the site where they were assembled into the house. The corner blocks posed a problem, until Bodil, a structural engineer, devised a method to cast them in place.

Unlike the later Usonian Automatics, which had coffered block ceilings, the Pieper house roof was of standard two-by-four wood framing with a ceiling of beveled Cemestos panels (a combination of cement and asbestos). This experimental house also differed from later versions in another critical respect—only one thickness of block was used for the walls. With no insulation in either the roof or the walls, the house became easily overheated in the blazing Arizona sun, particularly since it had no air-conditioning. Subsequent Usonian Automatics would use two blocks sandwiched together with air space in between forming natural insulation for the ceiling and walls.

Wright sited the house diagonally northwest to southeast on what was then an isolated stretch of desert at the base of the Phoenix Mountains. Spectacular views would have been visible from nearly every room. The in-line plan consisted of two bedrooms, one bath, a combined living and dining room, and a small kitchen. A carport and workshop extended the building to the northwest. The entryway, tucked between the kitchen and bedrooms, led straight through the house to a wall of tall glass doors and an open terrace. There, a panorama of pristine desert landscape would have greeted Arthur and Bodil in those early years. Today, the view is into the kitchen and dining room of the new house. Indeed, the addition so overshadows the small Pieper residence that a passerby might easily assume the original had been demolished.

BOOMER RESIDENCE

1953 PHOENIX, ARIZONA

With its soaring roofline and generous windows, the Boomer house resembles a tilted hat shading the interior from the desert sun. No wonder Wright called it the "Phoenix Sunbonnet."

THE STEEPLY PITCHED ROOF and expansive windows of the Boomer residence sweep skyward toward views of Squaw Peak by day and the North Star by night. Anchored to the earth by thick slabs of desert masonry, this fourteen-hundred-square-foot cottage of redwood, stone, and glass was originally conceived for a far different setting—an ocean site near Carmel, California. Wright often returned to earlier abandoned schemes, reworking and tailoring them for new clients. For Jorgine Boomer, a native New Yorker with a passion for the desert, he transformed a California beach house into a desert dwelling and proudly rechristened it the "Phoenix Sunbonnet."

Jorgine Boomer and her husband, Lucius, manager of the Waldorf Astoria Hotel in New York, had originally contacted Wright in 1945 about rebuilding the burned-out remains of the Pauson residence, Wright's first residential commission in Arizona. Designed in 1939 for Rose and Gertrude Pauson, the house was destroyed by fire just two years after it was finished. Though the redwood superstructure was gone, the extensive desert rubblestone base remained, and Wright hoped to see the house reconstructed. He successfully convinced the Pauson sisters to sell their property and the ruins of the house, but the untimely death of Lucius Boomer convinced Jorgine that something smaller would be more suitable.

Though deeply disappointed at her decision, Wright dusted off plans for a California house, converting the design from an ocean-view bungalow to an Arizona cottage. He accomplished this chiefly by orienting the house away from the western sun, toward cooler, northeastern views of the desert landscape. He also carved out

accommodations for Jorgine Boomer's maid behind the chimney upstairs, turned a storeroom into a bedroom for the chauffeur, and added a walled garden next to the sitting room. The new house was positioned about a third of a mile from the Pauson ruins, which were left untouched.

Laid out on a diamond grid, the two-story Boomer house has few right angles. All walls, windows, and built-in light fixtures meet in intriguing obtuse and acute angles. By reinforcing a consistent motif, such as a diamond or triangular unit, Wright gave his buildings harmony and discipline. Yet he did not sacrifice individuality—each is a singular work of art, made

cohesive by a carefully chosen architectural grammar. Even the Boomer house roofline echoes the theme.

The lower level of the house encloses a compact sitting room, a kitchen, a bath, and a servant's room. The cozy sitting room, with its exposed timber beams and low redwood ceiling, is dominated by the masonry core, a massive, angular mosaic of concrete and desert stone. Rising through the center of the house, the masonry incorporates two hearths and the first- and second-story bathrooms within its walls. A narrow entry leads from the sitting room to the kitchen, windowless except for a narrow band of high clerestories framed in perforated boards. Redwood cabinetry and open shelving provide storage in the kitchen, with just enough wall space left over for a three-sided dining table.

A narrow winding staircase, so low one must cleave to the inside or stoop down, leads to the second floor and two bedrooms—one a grand bedroom/sitting room for Jorgine Boomer, the other a narrow space for the maid. In great contrast to the darker cavelike sitting room directly below, the master bedroom, with its nearly two-story wall of glass, is bathed in natural light. Mitered at an obtuse angle, the generous windows reach into the roofline.

Jorgine Boomer lived in her cottage only a few years before she donated it to the Phoenix Art Museum. Unable to maintain it or use it as an auxiliary site due to zoning restrictions, the museum sold it in 1963. The house, which once sat starkly alone on the bare desert floor, is now surrounded by thick plumes of desert vegetation, planted and carefully tended by the present owner. As late as the 1970s, there was still some hope that the ruins of the Pauson residence might be rebuilt. But in 1979, the rubble-stone walls were demolished to make way for a new road. One lone chimney mass remains, positioned as a gateway to the subdivision that holds Wright's Boomer and Adelman residences.

FAR LEFT Wright based the design of the Boomer house on a favorite motif—the diamond. Diamond-shaped redwood light fixtures and rough-hewn beams appear overhead in the living room. Below, the diamond grid is incised into the red concrete floor. A walled garden is located behind the seating area to the west.

LEFT In most of Wright's houses, the living room is the central focus, but here the master bedroom on the second floor is paramount. In the evening, the entire arc of the star-filled northern sky can be seen through the floor-to-ceiling wall of glass.

ABOVE Like a tree whose cantilevered branches protect those who sit beneath it, the complex roof of the Boomer house shields the interior, creating a sense of privacy.

LEFT A lapped redwood balcony wraps around the second-floor master bedroom. Wright's diamond-shaped theme plays out even in the roofline.

PRICE RESIDENCE

1954 PARADISE VALLEY, ARIZONA

FRANK LLOYD WRIGHT CALLED IT the "Grandma House." From one end of its 170-foot length to the other, this large-scale, elegant house was designed to comfort and entertain the grandchildren of Harold and Mary Lou Price. Extremely long and narrow, the five-thousand-square-foot house has seven bedrooms, a living and dining area, a kitchen, and a carport all laid end to end, like the cars of a train. At the center is the main attraction, a one-thousand-square-foot atrium open to the sky and nature. Here, in this grand playroom, the Price grandchildren had the luxury of easy access to the desert, with complete privacy and protection from its prickly dangers.

Wright lavished a great deal of time and attention on this house for a favorite client. After all, it was Harold Price who gave Wright his only chance to build a skyscraper—the Price Tower in Bartlesville, Oklahoma.

FAR LEFT Wright gave form to his credo that a "desert building should be nobly simple in outline" in this house for Harold and Mary Lou Price. Set in the rugged landscape of the upper Sonoran Desert, the house, viewed from the southeast, extends in two directions from the central atrium. Tall masonry columns and a roof that appears to float on air create the drama and nobility Wright was seeking.

LEFT A splashing fountain, cool and refreshing in the desert, greets visitors at the entrance loggia. The stamped copper fascia with decorative cutouts and chips of turquoise lends elegance to the simple concrete block. Narrow steel pipes trimmed in turquoise-colored wooden cubes support the loggia roof.

During one of their many visits to Arizona to confer about the tower, Harold and Mary Lou Price decided to build a winter home in the desert, one with enough bedrooms to accommodate their grandchildren and a large master bedroom for themselves. Wright selected concrete block and steel as the main building components. Time, not cost, was the main objective: the owners wanted to take occupancy within eight months of the start of construction.

Being close at hand at his Taliesin West residence, Wright often dropped by the construction site in Paradise Valley, about ten miles away. No detail was too small to be undeserving of his attention, and he ordered countless alterations. But he failed to make the master bedroom large enough to suit Harold Price. Several years after it was finished, at Price's insistence, Wright converted the children's play yard into a twenty-by-forty-foot master bedroom suite.

From the sixty-foot-long walkway leading to the entrance, the grand scale of the house is not yet apparent. But after entering the atrium's eastern portico, the extraordinary vertical thrust of the imposing space makes it quite clear that this is not a typical dwelling, even for Wright. Massive concrete block piers, arranged like sentinels around an ancient altar, encircle the room. Narrow at the bottom, they flare out as they reach skyward, and then abruptly end just short of the powerful slablike roof. Thin steel pipes, festooned with turquoise-colored wooden cubes, lead the rest of the way, creating the illusion that the roof is floating on air.

Exquisitely crafted mahogany shutters adorned in brilliant jewel and metallic tones are set between the piers. Created by Eugene Masselink, Wright's longtime associate and assistant, the shutters are works of art in themselves. When they are

FAR LEFT Wright believed that all elements of a house—from furnishings to floor plan—should form a cohesive design. At the Price house he was given an ample budget and free rein to implement this philosophy. Wright created most of the furnishings, which in the combined living and dining room included upholstered chairs, brass lighting fixtures, mahogany tables, and built-in shelving and cabinetry. The turquoise color scheme is also his.

LEFT TOP The kitchen adjoins the dining area and is equipped with a mahogany work table with pull-out stools for conversation or simple meals. Countertops are stainless steel. The ceiling here and throughout the house is made of excelsior, a combination of straw and concrete that serves to soundproof and insulate the structure.

LEFT BOTTOM Four bedrooms extend from the atrium, grouped in pairs to form interconnected suites. A hallway forms when all doors are open between rooms.

BELOW Bedrooms are outfitted with built-in mahogany beds, tables, chests, and brass lights. High clerestories add daylight, yet ensure privacy when the hand-crafted shutters are closed.

RIGHT The desert is never far away, yet blends beautifully with the sculptural nature of the house.

FAR RIGHT On the cooler, northern side of the house, Wright provided a grassy court with flower beds and a play yard for the Prices' grandchildren. The children's bedrooms stretch out along this wing.

open, the room appears to merge with the desert landscape. When closed, they protect the room's inhabitants from the inhospitable desert wind. A copper fountain with a lighted basin occupies the center of the room. Above it, a square oculus, or skylight, opens to the sky. When rain falls, as it does even in this desert setting, it plunges straight down into the appropriately placed basin. A copper-hooded fireplace with a circular hearth is situated in the east corner of the room, providing warmth on chilly winter days.

The house expands in two directions from this central space. The bedroom wing extends to the northeast; the combined living room and dining area and the kitchen lead off to the southwest. Grouped in pairs to form interconnected suites, the four smaller rooms in the bedroom wing are amply outfitted with built-in mahogany closets and desks. Mahogany shutters cover the abundant north-facing casement windows. These built-in furnishings are complemented by Wright-designed mahogany beds, chests, and chairs. The master bedroom, at the northeastern terminus of the house, is separated from the other rooms for privacy and quiet. At the opposite end of the house, a detached wing contains two small guest rooms, two baths, and a carport large enough for four automobiles.

Wright originally planned a brown and berry red color scheme for the decorative steel elements and metal window mullions. When that proved unsuitable with the gray concrete block, Wright changed it to turquoise. To get the perfect blue-green shade he wanted, Wright had Charles Montooth, the construction supervisor, take a turquoise stone ring to the paint manufacturer to duplicate the color. Serendipitously, the entire color scheme was unified by a rare weather occurrence in the Arizona desert: two foggy nights back to back began the oxidation process that turned the copper fascia at the roofline to a lovely pale blue.

Pale lozenges of amber light spill across the living room floor, their form echoed by the coffered ceiling above. High, narrow windows above the built-in seating area ensure privacy on the north, while a wall of glass to the west opens onto views of Puget Sound below.

TRACY RESIDENCE

1955 NORMANDY PARK, WASHINGTON

MORE LIKE A FINE SCULPTURE than a family home, the Tracy residence nestles into a wooded bluff overlooking the sparkling waters of Puget Sound far below. Composed of seventeen hundred handcrafted concrete blocks, this jewel-like house is one of the most exquisite examples of the Usonian Automatic, Wright's experimental concept for moderate-cost, owner-built homes. A variation on his Usonian homes of the 1930s and 1940s, the Automatics, built during the 1950s, are a modular design composed of precast concrete blocks woven together with steel rods. But they were often neither low-cost nor particularly easy to build. Time-consuming and complicated, they frequently strained the stamina and patience of their owners.

The Tracys spent nearly a year, working five days a week, casting the eleven different types of blocks needed for their twelve-hundred-square-foot house—standard blocks, corner blocks, cutout window blocks, parapet blocks, and coffered blocks, just to name a few. Each backbreaking block weighed between 150 and 180 pounds. Twice a day they filled the steel molds, sanding and refinishing each block after it was removed from the form. When enough blocks were made, their contractor, Ray Brandes (owner and builder of the Wright-designed Brandes house), rented a truck with a hydraulic tailgate to move them to the construction site where they were assembled into a three-bedroom, one-story house.

Walking through these vibrant spaces today, it is apparent that the Tracys' efforts paid off. The crisp, clean lines of the perfectly crafted blocks are evident in the walls, ceilings, partitions, and garden walls, even the fireplace. Their crystalline beauty is particularly showcased in the lacy grid of window blocks that form nearly invisible piers on the western wall. Supporting a bold, flat roof, these piers frame three sets of French doors and corner glass doors that swing open from the living and dining area to spectacular views of Puget Sound. "Now the outside may come inside and the inside may and does go outside," Wright said. "They are of each other."

From this vantage point, it seems as if the house embraces the whole outdoors. But on the eastern side, where Wright located the entry, the house asserts a more secure and impenetrable presence. Here, imposing walls of concrete block, with high, narrow windows, shield the interior from public scrutiny. Although it is clear that privacy is paramount, the house nevertheless reaches out to embrace the visitor through a layered arrangement of horizontal and vertical planes that step gradually down toward the entrance drive.

Wright laid out most of his Usonian houses in what he called a polliwog plan, with the living room and kitchen as the body and the bedrooms as the tail. The size of the tail depended on the number of the bedrooms: "If the tail gets too long, it may curve like a centipede," he said. Because the Tracys had a narrow city lot, Wright altered this concept a bit, coiling the tail, or bedrooms, tightly around the kitchen area, creating a snug and efficient arrangement. Each of the bedrooms is partially bermed into a hill on the east or

Corners evaporate when these tall glass doors swing open. The rich tones of the redwood sash are the perfect counterpoint to the gleaming concrete blocks.

ABOVE LEFT Low coffered ceilings, redwood paneling, and built-in shelving lend a cozy, restful air to this compact bedroom, one of three in the twelve-hundred-square-foot house. Light fixtures concealed within the bookshelves direct illumination downward.

ABOVE RIGHT A carport, a low garden wall, and red concrete steps spread in cascading levels toward the entrance drive. From this guarded vantage point, it is impossible to anticipate the stunning vista that will open before the visitor once inside.

south, with a narrow band of clerestory windows providing natural light. A low ceiling height—six foot, six inches—few windows, and walls of dark-toned redwood paneling make these rooms quiet, sheltered sanctuaries.

The living and dining area, by contrast, is open, spacious, and filled with natural light. Bordered on the west by a wall of glass doors, these spaces form a connecting **L** that revolves around a central hearth. Behind the dining area, a small, yet practical, kitchen reaches a height of eleven feet, six inches—five feet taller than the bedrooms. William Tracy built the redwood banquette and dining room chairs, which are covered in a cheerful yellow fabric. He also built the light fixtures, designed to be concealed within the bookshelves and piers. Thus hidden, they create the illusion that light is coming from the building itself.

ABOVE A corner fireplace of coffered blocks is open on two sides, one facing the dining room, the other the living room. Designed by Wright, the redwood dining table and chairs were handcrafted by William Tracy.

RIGHT With its flat roof floating on crystalline piers that dissolve into walls of glass, the Tracy house appears to defy enclosure.

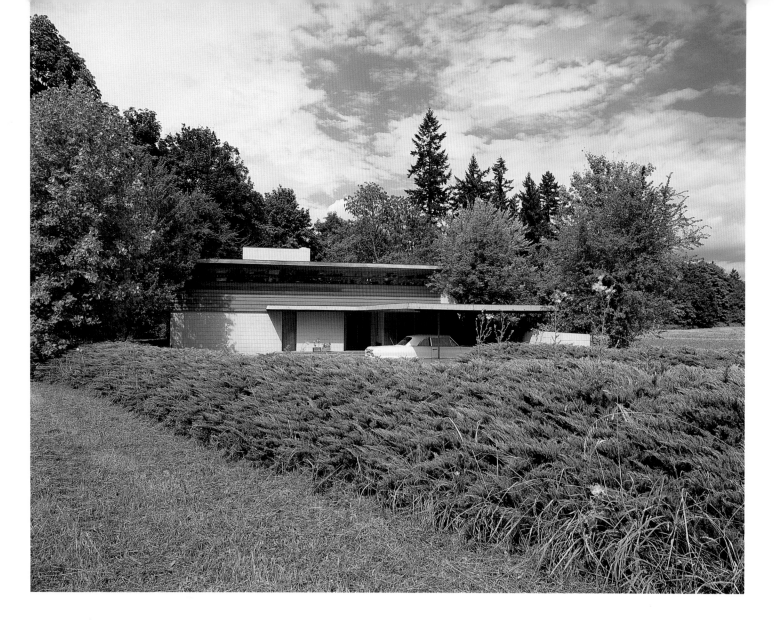

GORDON RESIDENCE

1956   WILSONVILLE, OREGON

THE TYPICAL AMERICAN HOME, Frank Lloyd Wright said, "was stuck up in a thoughtless fashion" with no sense of unity or concept of space. Whether of brick, wood, or stone, it was nothing more than a "fancy box with a fussy lid." Wright spent a lifetime in architecture attempting to break open this claustrophobic box and rip off its lid. For a farm couple in Oregon, he demonstrated that even at age eighty-nine he still had an extraordinary capacity to create fresh new architectural forms for the American family home.

LEFT The flat, bold planes forming the roof and cantilevered carport bring the two-story Gordon house into a close association with the earth. Wright invented the carport in the 1930s, a modest version of the elegant porte cochere he used in his Prairie Style houses at the turn of the century.

RIGHT The one-and-one-half story living room extends to outdoor terraces through glass doors opening to the east, here, and to the west. The perforated boards, on the right, shelter a compact dining area.

The Gordons' contact with Wright came about in 1956 when they visited Taliesin West during a trip to the Phoenix area. Wright's apprentices were often pressed into service as tour guides. When the Gordons mentioned their plans to build a house, their guide suggested that Wright might be interested in the commission. The Gordons were ushered into an impromptu meeting with the architect, who agreed to take on the project.

After studying photographs and topographical maps sent by the Gordons, Wright produced a bi-level, T-shaped plan of twenty-two hundred square feet. With no local stone available, he selected concrete block as the basic building material, and because of the damp Northwest climate, he chose treated red cedar for the soffits, balconies, and window sashes. From these natural materials, he created a harmonious design that eliminated all sense of confinement.

Wright's methods are particularly evident in the living room, where the dominant walls are composed of floor-to-ceiling glass windows and doors spaced rhythmically between narrow piers of concrete block. Embracing views of snowcapped Mount Hood to the east and the churning waters of the Willamette River to the west, these long parallel walls of glass appear more like screens than solid barriers. Overhead, a cantilevered flat roof floats above the piers, seemingly independent of the walls. A series of cutout squares punched into the deep eave over each window further accentuates the separation. By pulling apart the walls, eliminating unnecessary boundaries, and setting free the roof, Wright effectively "destroyed the box" both vertically and horizontally.

While Wright opened the living area to the surrounding views, he also provided a cozy inglenook by the fireplace as a point of seclusion and quiet comfort. Surrounded by an elegant arrangement of perforated wood panels, the space is warmed by a palette of red and the rich tones of wood. The delicate cutout shapes, layered one upon another, filter patterned light into the space and eliminate the need for further ornamentation. Wright balanced these decorative panels by incorporating a second set in the dining area alcove at the opposite end of the room.

The adjoining living and dining area, running north to south, forms the base of Wright's **T**-shaped plan. The two-story crossbar, running east to west, encloses the master bedroom, den, and kitchen below, with two bedrooms above. Each upstairs bedroom has its own private, cantilevered balcony, affording the early riser in the eastern room a commanding view of the sun rising over Mount Hood. On the first floor, the towerlike kitchen rises two stories. Natural light brightens the workspace from a skylight above. Daylight is brought into the upper reaches of the house through a third series of perforated boards set into clerestories at the roofline. During sunlit hours, delightful shadow patterns spill forth across the floor.

Despite its two-story height, the house retains an overwhelming sense of the horizontal. Cantilevered flat roofs that project over the walls seem to bring the house closer to the ground. From the south, parallel planes forming the carport and the second-story roof accentuate this horizontal thrust. Though the design was completed in 1956, financial considerations delayed construction until 1963.

Swept into the folds of Bountiful's North Canyon, the Stromquist residence belies its turbulent past. A provocative and unexpected shade of pale pink, the house surges forward on its sloping site.

STROMQUIST RESIDENCE

1958 BOUNTIFUL, UTAH

ALL OF THE FAMOUS PROPS were laid out when Donald and Jane Stromquist visited Frank Lloyd Wright at his home, Taliesin. His cape, cane, and porkpie hat were strewn across a table. A fire was burning in the fireplace and someone was playing a harp in a distant room. "Why, you're just a couple of kids," the ninety-year-old Wright said when they walked into his studio. He picked up a seashell and immediately launched into a lecture: "No one house should be like another," he told them. "Each should be like a seashell, beautiful and completely original."

Then he spread out the drawings for their new house, an exquisite dwelling of rock, glass, and mahogany with a tile roof, an atrium, and bedrooms swinging out in a separate wing toward the north. The Stromquists loved the design, but felt it would be too elaborate and costly for their lifestyle or budget. In a masterful stroke, Wright wrapped the bedrooms in snail-like fashion around the central core and changed the main building material from stone to concrete block, creating a design that was more compact and efficient, and less costly.

The Stromquists approved the new plan, and a year later, after Wright's death, Taliesin Architects completed the working drawings. Construction, under the firm's supervision, began in 1961. The site was spectacular and remote—a seven-acre stretch of canyon land high above Utah's most famous landmark, the Great Salt Lake. There was no water, no power, and no real road, so the Stromquists had to make provisions for their

own water system and generator. Wright's widow, Olgivanna, supervised the interior design, which was carried out by apprentice Cornelia Brierly. Donald Stromquist did his part by meticulously handcrafting and finishing all of the freestanding and built-in furnishings.

After spending only six years in his Wright-designed house, Don Stromquist was transferred by his employer, U.S. Steel, to offices in Pittsburgh. The company purchased the house and put it on the market, but no buyer could be found for this unusual and remote property, high above the canyon floor. In isolation, the house became a haven for transients, who warmed themselves by burning the precious woodwork and doors in the Wright-designed fireplace. The windows were broken and the water pipes burst.

Eventually, a new owner was found, but he had little sympathy for Wright's creation. Although the house was secured from the elements and made livable once again, it was not protected from the taste or hobbies of its new proprietor, who used it as a tack room and temporary stable. Shag carpet, flocked wallpaper, and a woodstove were installed, as were exterior hitching post rings to tether the owner's horses.

Today, all evidence of hippie haven and horse-barn have been erased. Lavishing great care and attention on their prize, new owners restored the twenty-seven-hundred-square-foot house to Wright's original specifications, a two-year process that began in 1989. Cornelia Brierly, who had helped with the original interiors, and John de Koven Hill, both of Taliesin Architects, guided the new owners in selecting new fabrics and furnishings for their restored house.

FAR LEFT The main entrance to the house is through this large door surrounded by glass on the northeast. The canted window mullions repeat Wright's angular theme for the house and echo the slope of the canyon wall. A previous owner's horse, tethered here for a while, managed to nibble away at the mahogany frame.

LEFT French doors set into a wall of glass on the north open to a triangular terrace and views of the Great Salt Lake far below. Banquettes upholstered in royal blue with accents of turquoise and pink enrich the interior. Hexagonal stools and taborets grouped in pleasing arrangements add to the house's unusual geometry. Overhead, tiny triangular lights are recessed into the ceiling.

The combination living room and dining area, as in most of Wright's domestic designs, is the centerpiece of the plan. The space soars toward generous windows and unimpeded views of the Great Salt Lake and Antelope Island to the northwest. Pale pink carpet, blue cushions, and turquoise pillows enliven the brightly lit space. Only a close examination of the fireplace yields evidence of the home's history as a horse barn: the iron grate is bent severely from being used as a forge. Of particular note in this room is the fenestration. Employed only one other time by Wright, in the Teater residence in Idaho, the window sash is slanted to mirror the sloping angle of the roof. Each framed window thus forms a tiny parallelogram, reinforcing the diamond module Wright chose for the house.

The workspace, or kitchen, is tucked into the masonry core, separating the bedrooms from the living room wing. There are no eye-level windows here, except for a shuttered opening that looks onto a corridor. Nonetheless, the tiny room gains amplitude and natural light from a high ceiling and a freestanding clerestory that rises above the main roofline, illuminating the space far below. A study, two small bedrooms, and a master bedroom with its own fireplace are arranged around the east and south end of the house. A private terrace off the master bedroom cantilevers over the canyon floor with views west. In the bedrooms, mitered glass walls join in 120-degree angles, dissolving the barrier between inside and out. In the evening, lit from within, this gem of glass and mahogany seems eminently suited to its new name: Crystalwood.

FAR LEFT The compact kitchen, set into the center of the house, is amply outfitted with built-in mahogany cupboards. The only eye-level window is the shuttered opening that looks onto the entry hall. Natural light reaches the workspace through clerestory windows far above.

MIDDLE Because the house has no gutters or downspouts, icicles accumulate in great crystal pendants. This strip of low windows looks from a bedroom into the backyard. The decorative mahogany fascia echoes the geometric theme Wright chose for the house.

LEFT A steep retaining wall of concrete block cleaves the Stromquist house to the hill. The sharply angled, cantilevered roof floats above the terrace like the lost wing of a great bird. Triangular masonry piers frame the structure and provide substance for walls of mitered glass. Most windows and walls meet in 60- or 120-degree angles.

Wright chose bricks of a variegated orange-tan hue for the clinic, with mortar tinted tan to match. To emphasize the building's horizontal thrust, he had the mortar raked a half inch deep on the horizontal joints and left flush on the vertical. A decorative white concrete fascia in a reverse curve contrasts with the warm wood and brick tones. The building's tallest element, a lapped board parapet which once held flowers and plants, is now marred by a **C**-shaped air-conditioning unit.

LOCKRIDGE MEDICAL CLINIC
1958 WHITEFISH, MONTANA

FRANK LLOYD WRIGHT DESIGNED a handful of medical buildings in his career including this clinic for Dr. T. L. Lockridge. Located in a remote area of northwest Montana, a scant fifty miles from the Canadian border, this glass, wood, and brick building did not remain a clinic long. Just one year after it opened, Dr. Lockridge died, and the structure was renovated into a bank. With the addition of a drive-up window and a rooftop air-conditioning unit, and the severe repartitioning of the interior, the building lost much of its original character. When the bank moved to new quarters in 1980, more changes were made. Today, one must look carefully to detect Wright's hand in the project.

Wright believed that good architecture could bring dignity and joy to everyday life. For Dr. Lockridge's patients, he demonstrated that this could be accomplished in a medical setting. In an atmosphere more reminiscent of a domestic living room than a doctor's office, Wright used warm colors and natural materials to impart a sense of serenity and comfort. A massive brick fireplace served as the focal point of the waiting room, with two built-in curved banquettes flanking the hearth to form an inglenook. Specially designed low tables for children were set near the windows, and the reception desk was kept small and unobtrusive to further enhance the homelike illusion. Natural light filled the space through a double clerestory window and a sixty-four-foot-long wall of floor-to-ceiling glass that faced west. Wright also engineered a pleasing view for Dr. Lockridge's patients by including plans for a landscaped garden to be filled with low bushes and colorful perennials.

LEFT At one time, a white plastic orb and a large brick planter pierced the long glass wall on the building's western side. All that is left now are two small arching planters composed of brick salvaged from the original planter.

RIGHT The central feature of the reception area was this elegant brick fireplace with an arching hearth. Originally, built-in curved banquettes flanked either side of the fireplace, with small round tables positioned near each end. After the building was converted from a medical clinic to a bank and other offices, the seating was removed, and a wooden mural of a western scene was placed over the hearth.

Examination rooms, nurses' stations, an X-ray unit, and other medical services were placed on either side of the waiting area. The north wing, where Dr. Lockridge maintained his office, included several consultation rooms and a space for minor surgery, accessible on two sides by means of double galleries or corridors. On the south, the building widened to provide space for the nurses' work area and a "shot room." Skylights brought natural light into these areas, while still ensuring necessary privacy.

There is one intriguing element in this design that appears to be without precedent in Wright's work: a seven-foot-diameter plastic sphere poised in the center of the glass wall facing the garden. Half inside and half outside the glass wall, this voluptuous white orb was supported by a twenty-five-foot-diameter brick planter, which also bisected the wall. Lit from below by floodlights, the glowing translucent bubble must have appeared almost otherworldly.

Construction of the five-thousand-square-foot clinic began in 1961, two years after Wright's death. With so many other pressing Wright projects to oversee, Taliesin Architects was unable to dispatch someone to Montana to supervise construction of the clinic. Instead a Whitefish carpenter traveled to Taliesin West to be "schooled" in Wright's methods.

Today, little remains of Wright's interior plan, save for the fireplace mass, now crowded by offices and half walls built within the original waiting room. The white orb and round brick planter are gone too, the casualties of Halloween pranksters and a careless driver who slammed into the low brick wall. Only the exterior of the long, low building retains a few of Wright's trademark touches: mitered glass windows, decorative white concrete fascia, and deep eaves.

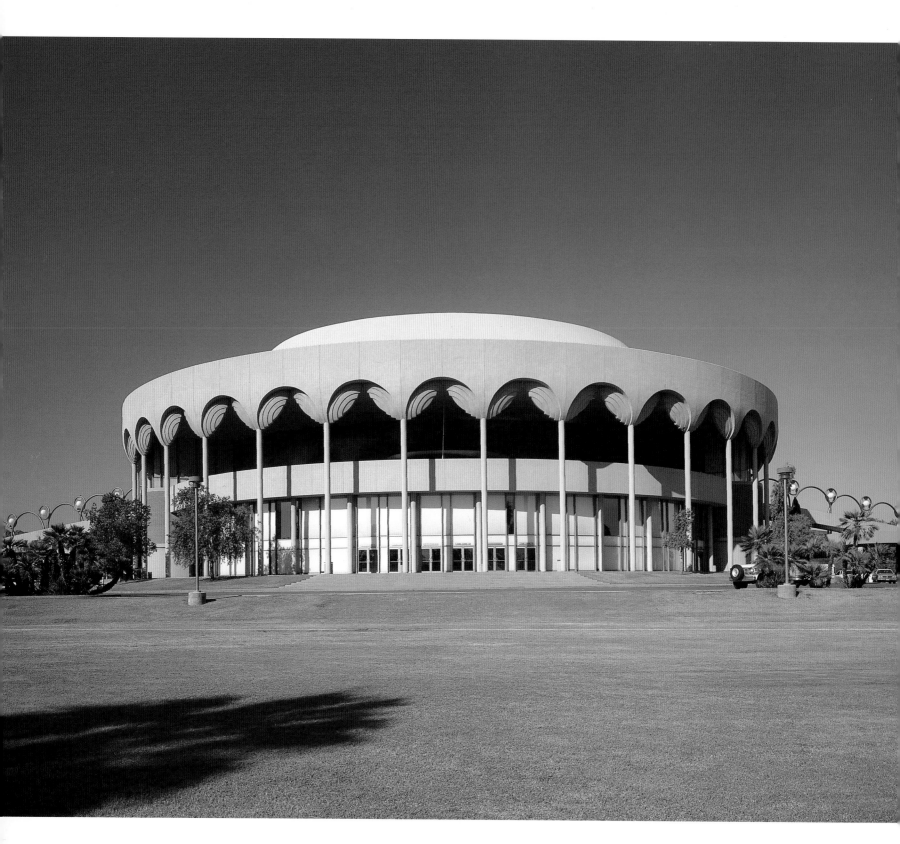

Encircled by forty-six slender pink columns, the main rotunda of the auditorium seats three thousand theater patrons on three levels. Pedestrian bridges stretch out from the building's second story like welcoming arms. Fifty-seven shades of pink—from deep terra-cotta to pale rose—are said to be used on the structure.

GRADY GAMMAGE MEMORIAL AUDITORIUM

1959 TEMPE, ARIZONA

IN THE LAST DECADES of his life, Frank Lloyd Wright experimented with a variety of unconventional geometric grids. Hexagons, diamonds, triangles, and circles were employed to create a vast array of complex architectural forms. Among these, the circle may have offered Wright his most fluid and daring geometry. At Grady Gammage Memorial Auditorium, Wright merged two circular forms to create a building in the shape of a figure eight. Provocative in color and form, this graceful structure makes a striking entrance to the Arizona State University campus. The dominant rotunda, composed of steel, concrete, and plaster in a delicate shade of pale rose, encompasses an expansive foyer and a three-thousand-seat performing arts auditorium. The smaller circle of brick with rose-tinted mortar encloses the stage, classrooms, and rehearsal space.

Originally designed as an opera house for Baghdad, Iraq, the building was to be part of an elaborate cultural and educational center commissioned by the Iraqi government to enhance the ancient capital. Wright traveled to Baghdad in May of 1957 and was motivated by what he saw to develop a plan he felt reflected the local culture and history. He was particularly drawn to the Arabian tales, *One Thousand and One Nights,* which inspired a fanciful and elaborate circular design. The overthrow of the government the next year, however, dashed Wright's hope of leaving a lasting mark on the Iraqi desert landscape.

LEFT During intermission, theater patrons can step out onto this upper-level balcony beneath the "butterfly wing" capitals to catch a breath of fresh air and views of the desert to the south.

At about the same time Wright was conjuring designs for Baghdad, Grady Gammage, a longtime friend and president of Arizona State University, was privately dreaming of a truly distinctive university auditorium for the A.S.U. campus. At one point, he shared his thoughts with Wright, and the two walked the entire width and breadth of the campus searching for a site. After contemplating a grassy lawn bordered by a curving highway, Wright declared that the structure should be circular "with outstretched arms saying 'Welcome to Arizona!'"

It is unclear whether Wright had the opera house in mind when he suggested a circular design to Gammage. Nevertheless, Wright eventually saw this as an opportunity to transplant the Baghdad design from one desert oasis to another. Neither man lived to see the building take shape. Thus it fell to Wright's successor firm, Taliesin Architects, particularly William Wesley Peters and John Rattenbury, to complete the commission. After Gammage's death, the university chose to name the building in his honor.

The grandiose facade of Grady Gammage Memorial Auditorium gives the illusion of amplitude and grace, an image enhanced by a towering colonnade of forty-six slender concrete and steel columns that encircle the main rotunda. Rising fifty-five feet to support the outer roof, each column is topped by an

ABOVE The smaller brick rotunda encloses the stage and four floors of classrooms for Arizona State University's School of Music. Rose-tinted mortar, colored to match the brick, was raked three-quarter inch deep horizontally, but kept flush vertically, to enhance the roundness of the structure. Individual bricks seem to disappear, creating the illusion of carved stone. Narrow half-moon windows encircle the structure at the second-story level.

BELOW Lighted white plastic spheres suspended from copper-colored metalwork illuminate the pedestrian pathway that leads from the parking lot to the second-level balcony.

RIGHT The desert rose color scheme and curvilinear motif continue throughout the interior. The arched box office area is walnut, as is all the interior trim. Theater patrons ascend ramps to the grand tier and balcony on the second and third level.

BELOW The interior abounds with circular shapes—the water fountains, air ducts, light fixtures, and even the walnut phone booths are round.

oversized capital, described variously as "butterfly wings" or "parted curtains." Behind the columns, a glistening thirty-foot-high wall of glass sweeps halfway around the structure, providing multiple entry points into the lobby.

The "outstretched arms" Wright spoke of—originally flying buttresses in the opera house—became a pair of two-hundred-foot-long pedestrian bridges that link the parking areas with the building's upper-level lobbies. These sloping, bi-level walkways flank the main rotunda and extend the building horizontally. A looping, copper-colored steel railing, punctuated by ten lighted spheres, adorns the top level of each bridge, a detail that differs from the delicate filigreed ornament suggested by Wright's original opera house drawings.

The interior of the vast auditorium, with its curving, undulating forms, seems almost sensuous. The shapely spaces enhance the acoustics, particularly the bowl-shaped second balcony, which is detached from the back wall and suspended on a 145-foot-long steel girder. Sound can thus roll around the balcony, bouncing back to even the most remote seats. Acoustics are further strengthened by the ceiling—a continuous piece of sprayed concrete plaster which scallops back from the stage to the rear of the house. Taliesin Architects designed all interior spaces including the auditorium, lobby, rehearsal areas, and classrooms.

GRADY GAMMAGE MEMORIAL AUDITORIUM

LYKES RESIDENCE

1959 PHOENIX, ARIZONA

FRANK LLOYD WRIGHT NEVER touched pencil to paper without having a design concept fully worked out in his mind. And when he did, floor plans, elevations, and sections would come pouring forth. One landmark day in 1956, as his apprentices recall, Wright designed the Annunciation Greek Orthodox Church for Milwaukee, Wisconsin, in the morning and the proposed Mile High Skyscraper for Chicago in the afternoon. Among the last sketches to come from Wright's hand in 1959 was a pencil study of a house dramatically perched on a craggy promontory. Wright apprentice John Rattenbury sat at the architect's side as he sketched two embracing circles and described the general plan.

"Here is the living room, with a view over the valley," Wright said. "The bedrooms will wrap around the hillside, on the far side of the house. Every room will have a view." As he continued to draw, Wright kept up his running commentary, relating how the house would look, and also imagining how Norman and Aimee Lykes would live there. "Let's give them a garden court where they can be outdoors," he said, "with a wall around them

A low masonry wall punctuated by cutout circles and triangles offers framed views of the desert landscape, while creating a sense of privacy around the pool. Squaw Peak rises to the north, behind the house.

giving them privacy. They can look upwards, over the court wall, and see the surrounding mountains." After a while, Wright got up from his desk and walked out of the studio, never to return to the drawings again. The next week, on April 9, 1959, he died just two months shy of his ninety-second birthday.

Keeping in mind Wright's commentary and following his plan, Rattenbury finished the presentation drawings and showed them to the clients. They were thrilled with the design, but decided to wait until a more favorable time to build. Seven years later, they proceeded, making the Norman Lykes house Wright's last residential design to be constructed by the client who commissioned the work. Rattenbury supervised the construction and designed the furnishings, both built-in and freestanding pieces, which were handcrafted from Philippine mahogany.

Set into a natural plateau at the southern edge of a rocky slope high above the desert floor, the Lykes house closely follows the contour lines of its dramatic site. Constructed of a buff-colored concrete block, the three-thousand-square-foot residence wraps around the mountain, trapping the prevailing breezes beneath its deep eaves. Sleek and modern, the house appears futuristic, yet is "integral to site, integral to the environment, and integral to the life of the inhabitants," as Wright described the key concepts of his organic architecture.

Two circular drumlike pavilions, separated by a curved bedroom wing, form the nucleus of the house.

A drumlike tower with a small concave balcony encloses the master bedroom, which is connected to the main living space by a curved bedroom wing. Set into a plateau near the top of Squaw Peak, the house opens to spectacular views of the city below.

The living area, in the main pavilion, is a chorus of interlocking circular shapes. Built-in seating at the circumference thwarts the natural inclination to move to the center of the room. Narrow wrap-around windows offer views south toward cactus-studded foothills and the miniature Phoenix skyline far below. The quality of light is enhanced by a band of clerestory windows at the roofline, which bounce captured daylight off projecting decks and into the room. Indirect-lighting fixtures are also embedded into these decks, creating the illusion that the artificial light comes from the same source as the natural light.

A doorway to the right of the living room fireplace leads to a circular workspace, or kitchen. Playful half-moon windows beneath tall mahogany cabinets reinforce Wright's exuberant geometric theme. Above the kitchen, at the top of the drum, is a private study with a second tier of half-moon windows.

Arching out from the living room, the bedroom wing terminates in the master bedroom and bath. All of the bedrooms open out to the view, including the master bedroom, which has a small, concave balcony facing south. Although the Lykes House opens out to the sky, the landscape, and the light, broad roof overhangs provide a sense of protection and shelter. From the outside, the windows appear as if they are merely tiny slices of glass; inside they open onto grand vistas. This is a hallmark of Wright's design philosophy: creating a sense of shelter that encloses yet does not confine.

Aimee Lykes lived in the house for nearly twenty years and then rented it to a succession of tenants who seemed to care little for the property. In 1994, the house was sold to a new owner, who meticulously refurbished it, reversing years of damage and making the house very much her own statement on how to live in a Wright dwelling.

RIGHT A covered entryway rings the back of the house, which hugs close to the mountainside on the north.

FAR RIGHT Half-circle windows dance around the cylinder that holds a kitchen on the ground floor and a bedroom/study above. A curved wall of sliding glass doors opens from the living room onto the pool area.

JESTER-PFEIFFER RESIDENCE

1938/1971 SCOTTSDALE, ARIZONA

One must set aside all ordinary ideas of
what a house should be when ascending
the wide red platform and shallow steps
that lead to the gated entrance of the
Jester-Pfeiffer house. A sharp, horizontal
plane, trellised over the entry, serves as a
roof.

SET BENEATH THE LOWEST FOOTHILL of the McDowell Mountains in northeastern Scottsdale, a series of pale beige cylinders rises vertically from a low red platform. These curving towers, smooth, tall, and round, are the heart of a house Wright designed in 1938 for Hollywood set designer Ralph Jester. A welcome contrast to the thorny desert brush and spare landscape that surrounds it, this graceful home was a new concept for Wright, his first residential work based entirely on a circular motif. Wright would return to this theme many times in his career in such buildings as the Annunciation Greek Orthodox Church in Milwaukee, the house in Phoenix for his son David, and in his most eloquent expression of the circular form, the Solomon R. Guggenheim Museum in New York.

     Jester, who worked with Hollywood producer Cecil B. DeMille as a set designer for Paramount Studios, asked Wright to design a house for a narrow strip of California coastline with a distant view of the Pacific Ocean. "Have hit upon a nice scheme for your house," Wright wrote Jester in 1938, "a true abstraction." Jester responded confidently that he "should be able to live a very ethereal life in an abstraction," but high construction bids apparently forced him to abandon the plans. Never one to waste a good idea, Wright offered variations of this design to no fewer than nine clients over the next twenty years, but he found no takers. In 1971, twelve years after Wright's death, Bruce Brooks Pfeiffer, director of the Frank Lloyd Wright Archives and resident of Taliesin West since 1949, resurrected it from among Wright's unbuilt designs as a home for himself and his recently widowed father. Pfeiffer, who was trained as an architect by Wright, prepared the working drawings and developed the interior design.

The Jester-Pfeiffer house is not a house in any conventional sense. It is, instead, a series of drumlike spaces of varying height, widely spaced around a red concrete terrace. Each cylinder encloses a separate living area, with the outdoor space providing connecting exterior hallways. Arranged on a rectangular grid, these round pavilions are intersected overhead by a strongly defined horizontal platform that serves as a roof. One must go out of doors to move from room to room.

FAR LEFT, TOP The living room, at twenty-seven feet in diameter, is the largest cylinder in the plan. Curved built-in seating, large enough to accommodate twenty-five guests, follows the perimeter. A lighting deck, placed eight feet above the floor, provides space for books and artwork and brings the expansive room closer to human scale. Low, narrow windows ring the room, offering stunning views only to those who are seated. Reproductions of Wright-designed furnishings form several intimate zones for writing or reading.

FAR LEFT, BOTTOM Wright placed wide glass doors where the individual cylinders face the shady central patio, allowing easy access to the outside. The living room pavilion is on the right; the master bedroom straight ahead; and the kitchen and dining room on the left. The open patio offers a charming spot for informal meals.

LEFT A round, walk-in fireplace bulges into the living room, its solid walls contrasting with the clear glass panel that looks into a garden. A reproduction of Wright's Taliesin West chair is pulled up to the fire; his Midway Gardens chair and a hexagonal table are on the left.

The rugged foothills of the McDowell Mountains and lush native vegetation form a pleasant contrast to the supple, smooth forms of the Jester residence. The tall, narrow stack holds the vent for the kitchen stove. Pfeiffer added a two-car garage, nearly hidden on the left.

The two-thousand-square-foot house is entered from the west through a decorative steel gate that opens onto a central courtyard. This plant-filled atrium serves as informal dining area and open-air hallway. To the right is a suite of three connected drums of varying height that contain the dining room, kitchen, guest room, and bath. Straight ahead is the living room pavilion. To the left is the master bedroom and bath.

Each main cylinder is set with one side facing the shady patio and the other facing the Sonoran Desert landscape. Where the room intersects the patio, Wright placed wide expanses of glass or French doors, allowing free access to the garden atrium, yet shielding the interior from the direct sun. Where the room turns its face to the desert, a long, narrow band of windows, set below eye level, keeps the scorching sun at bay. At first these slot windows seem too small and low, until one sits down. Suddenly, a 270-degree panorama of stunning desert landscape springs into view, and one realizes that this moment was brilliantly choreographed by Wright, albeit for a different location.

Wright's original design called for curved laminated plywood with stone column masses and a stone fireplace. A large, round swimming pool, supported by a massive stone retaining wall, was to extend from the building's southern edge. But when transplanting the design to a desert climate, Pfeiffer chose instead cement and plaster on a two-by-four wood frame with concrete block column masses. To add texture to the plastered surfaces of the piers and fireplace mass, chips of flamingo quartz were embedded into the curved walls. He also added a carport to the design and increased the vertical scale of the house slightly. The large pool, too expensive and impractical for the desert, became a garden with a small plunge pool at the southern edge overlooking the desert and nearby foothills.

FIRST CHRISTIAN CHURCH

1950/1971   PHOENIX, ARIZONA

ABOVE A range of sawtooth clerestories inset with stained glass march down from the central spire to the eastern and western transept. The spire, which Wright called the "lantern," is also inset with glass, casting a shimmering multicolored glow in the evening. Wright designed the roof to be of copper, but high prices forced the congregation to select a pale blue urethane covering that simulates oxidized copper.

RIGHT There appear to be no walls within the sanctuary itself, only a series of sturdy columns placed at the building's perimeter, with asymmetrical clear glass windows marking the barrier between inside and out. The gold-tinted ceiling is pierced from east to west by a raised rib of jewel-toned stained glass clerestories.

The freestanding 120-foot tower on the east was constructed in 1978 of concrete, desert stone, and steel. The cross alone is twenty-two feet high. Below the tower, a colonnade of pillars connected by a lacy concrete arbor shields the interior of the church from the harsh desert sun.

Wright once remarked that he spelled god with a capital N for Nature, because that was "all we would ever really see of god." His ecumenical outlook, and ability to translate the philosophy and traditions of almost any denomination into stone and mortar, enabled him to design some thirty religious buildings during his career. The three-sided pillars reflect the triangular motif Wright chose for First Christian Church, a theme meant to reflect the concept of the Christian Trinity.

"CHURCHES INTEREST ME," Frank Lloyd Wright said in 1958. "It's not [only] because I am an architect, but because I am a son, a grandson—and also a great grandson—of preachers." Harmony, truth, beauty, freedom, and, above all else, a belief in oneself were instilled in the young Wright by his Unitarian forebears. These precepts furnished him with a lifelong philosophy and the basis by which to approach the design of nearly thirty religious buildings during his career. Wright's first completed design was, in fact, a church—the interior of his family's country chapel in Wisconsin, built in 1886 when "the boy architect" was only nineteen. Wright came to believe that the most important element in church design was a reverence for the beautiful. "If your church isn't beautiful," he said simply, "tear it down." When he wrote those words, in 1958, plans for a Jewish synagogue, a Greek Orthodox church, and a Christian Science church were at various stages on his drafting table.

Wright's most ambitious ecclesiastical commission came in 1949, when Dr. Peyton Canary, president of the Southwest Christian Seminary in Phoenix, asked him to prepare plans for a complete Christian university. The eighty-acre campus was to include a chapel, administrative buildings, seminar rooms, a library, a Greek theater, and faculty housing—just the kind of all-encompassing project that Wright enjoyed. He prepared an extensive set of elevation and presentation drawings in 1950, but financial setbacks forced the seminary to abandon the project.

The drawings languished in Wright's studio for some twenty years, until the Rev. William S. Boice, who had once worked with Dr. Canary, remembered the design. After determining that Wright's plans were still available, Dr. Boice successfully convinced his congregation, First Christian Church of Phoenix, that the university

chapel would be perfect for its needs. Under the direction of William Wesley Peters, chief architect of Taliesin Architects, which carried on Wright's work after his death in 1959, the building began to take shape in northeast Phoenix in 1971. Twenty tons of stone were gathered from the desert floor near Wright's home, Taliesin West, to build the rubblestone walls and ceiling of the church. The roof was to be of copper, but when this proved too costly for the congregation, Peters suggested a pale blue urethane to simulate oxidized copper.

First Christian Church embraces Wright's belief that the modern church building should be based on "new styles attuned to the new day." Taking the horizontal line as the "true earth-line of human life," Wright created a low, complex, asymmetrical design that sweeps north to south across its grassy ten-acre site. Unlike the Gothic cathedrals of old,

The angular roof slopes gently toward the ground, yet where it engages the building, it seems to hover above the masonry and glass walls. A tier of small, fluted columns with clerestory windows between them creates this illusion. When Wright originally unveiled the plan in 1950, he declared, "Here comes to Phoenix the new 'religious' architecture. The free, happy integral architecture of the new church of man."

wherein man was made to feel insignificant by a soaring, imposing structure, the First Christian Church, grounded to the earth, inspires and comforts man at the same time that it exalts God.

Although Wright rejected historical forms for modern buildings, he nevertheless respected the ancient traditions of each faith, believing that a church should reflect the philosophy of its parishioners. Thus, in developing his plans for the Christian university, Wright chose the triangle as the basic design module, a shape he said represented both a building in an attitude of prayer and the Christian Trinity. Most of the building's complex shapes—windows, walls, and sloping pyramidal roof—are based on the triangle. The twenty-three pillars of concrete and steel that support the building are triangular in outline. Even the building itself, as revealed in the plan, is a vast irregular diamond shape, or two equilateral triangles placed back-to-back.

Wright did not envision the need for a baptistry or a choir loft when designing the original university chapel. These were added by Taliesin Architects. The choir loft was placed in a gallery above the narthex; the baptistry, behind the pulpit. The interior color scheme of gold and blue was selected by Wright's widow, Olgivanna Wright. At her suggestion, turquoise carpeting covers the floor and the pews. The church seats eight hundred parishioners, all on one level.

In 1978 the congregation added a freestanding bell tower from Wright's original design. Built of precast concrete panels and desert masonry, the angular tower rises up 120 feet from a narrow base. Topped by a four-ton gold cross, the four-sided tower appears from any vantage point to be triangular. Administrative offices, classrooms, library, meeting rooms, and music rehearsal facilities are located in a north wing that was added in 1979, completing Wright's plan for the church.

POTTERY HOUSE
1942/1985 Santa Fe, New Mexico

LEFT An immense, potlike barrel serves as a fireplace for the Pottery House and holds two hearths, one open to the living room (top photo), the other to the courtyard. In the courtyard, the barrel's full height can be seen as it breaks through the roofline. In the living room it engages a ceiling composed of lapped boards of Douglas fir, curved to match the outline of the house. The stucco-covered barrel is poised atop a tiny perch of corbeled bricks.

ABOVE Two curving wings of stucco-covered adobe wrap around a central courtyard, forming the basic structure of the Pottery House. To the right is the bedroom and living room wing; to the left, the dining room, kitchen, and study. A red brick pathway leads from an outer gateway to the living room entrance behind the barrel fireplace. Originally all rooms were meant to open directly onto the courtyard, but the Sante Fe climate required the addition of the glass-enclosed corridor on the right.

Double rows of clay drain pipes set into the middle of the bulging adobe wall were meant to serve as fresh air ducts in Wright's original plan. Though the house is air-conditioned, architect Charles Montooth retained the pipes as an important decorative link to the original. Below the pipes, he added a low window, which looks toward mountain views.

FRANK LLOYD WRIGHT RESPONDED to newspaperman Lloyd Burlingham's 1942 request for a house design with typical ingenuity. For a ridge northwest of El Paso, Texas, he produced a design that perfectly suited the region's barren landscape and kept the harsh desert winds at bay. The result was an arc-shaped plan composed of two curved wings enclosing a garden—or as Wright described it, "a patio surrounded by a house." The sweeping sands and arid climate suggested adobe as the main building material, and Wright, associating adobe with pottery, thereafter referred to it as the Pottery House. The Burlinghams liked the design, but World War II intervened and the drawings were shelved.

Forty-five years later, a developer paging through a book discovered the design among a group of Wright's unbuilt works. Intrigued by the notion of building a Wright-designed adobe, he commissioned Taliesin Architects to adapt the house for a site overlooking Santa Fe, where adobe houses are common. Architect Charles Montooth updated the design to meet the client's needs, which in this case meant enlarging the house fifty percent from its original two thousand square feet. Since Wright based the design on a radial grid of concentric arcs, Montooth accomplished this feat by simply increasing the space between the arcs.

Low to the ground with stucco-covered adobe walls that bulge in the middle, the structure more clearly resembles a giant terra-cotta pot than a house. Clay drain pipes set in a double row create a decorative pattern along the pot's upper belly. Entry is gained through a gated portal on the east, which opens onto a sunny courtyard sheltered by the two curved wings that form the house. One wing holds the living room and three bedrooms. The other contains the dining room, breakfast nook, kitchen, and study. The wings meet at narrow

ABOVE The house is entered beneath a trellised opening on the left leading to an open courtyard. The bulging pink walls resemble a giant terra-cotta pot.

RIGHT An eye-shaped portal is carved into the thick wall, offering a glimpse into the garden courtyard and master bedroom. The walls are composed of twenty-four thousand adobe blocks covered in stucco.

points, facing due north and south. Most rooms open into the flagstone courtyard, where poplar trees grow and ornamental koi fish are kept in a narrow pond that hugs the eastern arc. Outside the house, a low retaining wall rings the perimeter, crowded by the ubiquitous piñon pines, junipers, and aspen that blanket the countryside. There is very little lawn; instead half-circle terraces on the east and west open the house to broad views of distant mountains.

Twenty-four thousand adobe bricks form the walls, which are concave on the outside, but are engineered to be vertical on the interior, though some inside walls also curve. Doorways and windows carved into the adobe create deep, shadowed reveals. Montooth specified Douglas fir for the ceiling boards, window sashes, and cabinetry. The floor is of red brick, which flows from inside the house to outside terraces and curving walkways. At the client's request, Montooth reduced the original four bedrooms to three,

using the extra space to expand the bathrooms. He added a swimming pool where a garden was intended, carved a breakfast nook from a corner of the dining room, and turned a service area into a study and an extra bathroom. One of the most unusual changes is the addition of a narrow waterway that leads from the bathroom directly to the pool, making it possible to swim to the outdoor pool from inside the house.

It is a difficult balancing act to bring a Wright design to life and yet remain true to the master architect's philosophy. Changes inevitably must be made to bring the buildings up to modern-day codes, and Wright's notoriously small bathrooms, kitchens, and bedrooms rarely meet the needs of today's clients.

Though the Pottery House is larger than Wright intended, its form, design concept, and materials are reminiscent of the original. It also represents an unusual design approach by Wright, that of completely enclosing a house around a central garden.

UNBUILT WORKS IN THE WEST

Many of Frank Lloyd Wright's best designs for the West were not built. Clients who changed their minds or divorced, the stock market crash, conservative bankers, and the shortages of World War II left much of Wright's most interesting and provocative work only ideas on paper. Below is a chronological list of some of these unrealized projects.

HORSESHOE INN, Estes Park, Colorado, 1908

BITTER ROOT TOWN PLAN, Darby, Montana, 1909

WENATCHEE TOWN PLAN, Wenatchee, Washington, 1919

RALPH AND WELLINGTON CUDNEY RESIDENCES, Chandler, Arizona, 1928

SAN MARCOS-IN-THE-DESERT RESORT, Chandler, Arizona, 1928

MRS. OWEN D. YOUNG RESIDENCE, Chandler, Arizona, 1928

SAN MARCOS GOLF CLUBHOUSE, POLO STABLES, WATER GARDENS, Chandler, Arizona, 1929

HOUSE ON THE MESA FOR GEORGE CRAMER, Denver, Colorado, 1931

CAPITOL JOURNAL OFFICE BUILDING AND NEWSPAPER PLANT, Salem, Oregon, 1931

LITTLE SAN MARCOS RESORT INN, Chandler, Arizona, 1936

MARGARET SCHEVILL RESIDENCE, Tucson, Arizona, 1941

ELIZABETH ARDEN SPA, Phoenix, Arizona, 1945

DR. PAUL V. PALMER RESIDENCE, Phoenix, Arizona, 1947

VALLEY NATIONAL BANK, Tucson, Arizona, 1947

MRS. WALTER BIMSON PENTHOUSE REMODELING, Phoenix, Arizona, 1948

METEOR CRATER INN, Meteor Crater, Arizona, 1948

LOUIS BLOOMFIELD RESIDENCE, Tucson, Arizona, 1949

ALAN DRUMMOND RESIDENCE, Santa Fe, New Mexico, 1949

SOUTHWEST CHRISTIAN SEMINARY, Phoenix, Arizona, 1950

RICHARD HANSON RESIDENCE, Corvalis, Oregon, 1950

MOBILE HOME PARK FOR LEE ACKERMAN, Phoenix, Arizona, 1952

PIEPER-MONTOOTH OFFICE BUILDING, Scottsdale, Arizona, 1953

ROBERT HERBERGER RESIDENCE, Maricopa County, Arizona, 1955

C. R. PIEPER RESIDENCE, Paradise Valley, Arizona, 1955

AIR FORCE ACADEMY, Boulder, Colorado, 1955

JAY ROBERTS RESIDENCE, Seattle, Washington, 1955

DAVID HUNT RESIDENCE, Scottsdale, Arizona, 1956

ARIZONA STATE CAPITOL, Phoenix, Arizona, 1957

USONIAN HOUSING PROJECT FOR WALTER BIMSON, Phoenix, Arizona, 1957

CARL HOYER RESIDENCE, Maricopa County, Arizona, 1957

DR. JAMES GUTIERREZ RESIDENCE, Albuquerque, New Mexico, 1958

ARIZONA STATE UNIVERSITY ART GALLERY, MASTER PLAN, MUSIC DEPARTMENT, RECITAL THEATER, Tempe, Arizona, 1959

HELEN DONAHOE RESIDENCE, Paradise Valley, Arizona, 1959

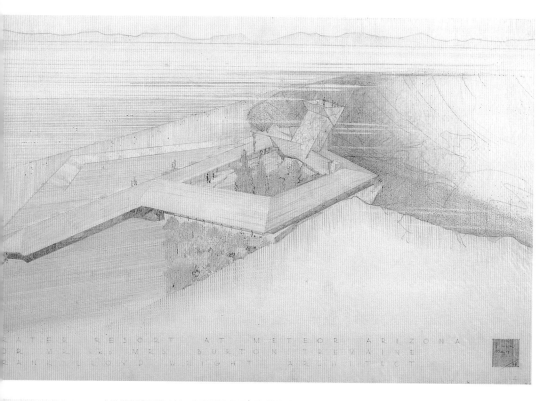

CRATER RESORT AT METEOR ARIZONA
FOR MR AND MRS BURTON TREMAINE
FRANK LLOYD WRIGHT ARCHITECT

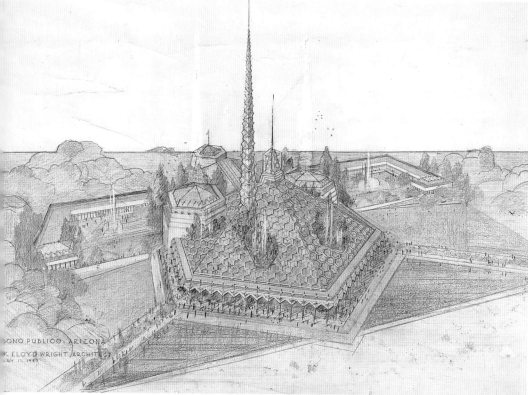

OSONO PUBLICO ARIZONA
FRANK LLOYD WRIGHT ARCHITECT

TOP Crater Resort, Meteor Crater, Arizona, 1948.

BOTTOM Arizona State Capitol, Phoenix, Arizona, 1957.

FURTHER READING

The following books discuss Frank Lloyd Wright's works in the West.

Dunham, Judith. *Details of Frank Lloyd Wright: The California Work, 1909-1974.* San Francisco: Chronicle Books, 1994.

Futagawa, Yukio, and Bruce Brooks Pfeiffer. *Frank Lloyd Wright, Monographs, Studies and Renderings. Vols. 1-12.* Tokyo: A.D.A. Edita, 1989.

——. *Frank Lloyd Wright Selected Houses 3, 8.* Tokyo: A.D.A. Edita, 1989.

Gebhard, David. *The California Architecture of Frank Lloyd Wright.* San Francisco: Chronicle Books, 1997.

Guerrero, Pedro. *Picturing Wright: An Album from Frank Lloyd Wright's Photographer.* San Francisco: An Archetype Press Book, Pomegranate Artbooks, 1994.

Hanks, David A. *The Decorative Designs of Frank Lloyd Wright.* New York: E. P. Dutton, 1979.

Levine, Neil. *The Architecture of Frank Lloyd Wright.* Princeton, N.J.: Princeton University Press, 1996.

Lind, Carla. *Frank Lloyd Wright's Usonian Houses.* San Francisco: An Archetype Press Book, Pomegranate Artbooks, 1994.

——. *Lost Wright: Frank Lloyd Wright's Vanished Masterpieces.* New York: An Archetype Press Book, Simon & Schuster, 1996.

Pfeiffer, Bruce Brooks. *Frank Lloyd Wright: The Masterworks.* New York: Rizzoli/Frank Lloyd Wright Foundation, 1993.

——. *Frank Lloyd Wright: In the Realm of Ideas.* Carbondale, Ill.: Southern Illinois University Press, 1988.

Secrest, Meryle. *Frank Lloyd Wright: A Biography.* New York: Alfred A. Knopf, 1992.

Sergeant, John. *Frank Lloyd Wright's Usonian Houses: The Case for Organic Architecture.* New York: Whitney Library of Design, 1976; Watson-Guptill Publications, 1984.

Smith, Kathryn. *Frank Lloyd Wright's Taliesin and Taliesin West.* New York: Harry N. Abrams, 1997.

Sweeney, Robert L. *Wright in Hollywood: Visions of a New Architecture.* New York: Architectural History Foundation, MIT Press, 1994.

Storrer, William Allin. *The Frank Lloyd Wright Companion.* Chicago: University of Chicago Press, 1993.

Wright, Frank Lloyd. *An Autobiography. Frank Lloyd Wright: The Collected Writings.* Edited by Bruce Brooks Pfeiffer. Vol. 2. New York: Rizzoli/Frank Lloyd Wright Foundation, 1992.

——. *An Autobiography. Book Five. Frank Lloyd Wright: The Collected Writings.* Edited by Bruce Brooks Pfeiffer. Vol. 4. New York: Rizzoli/Frank Lloyd Wright Foundation, 1994.

——. *The Natural House. Frank Lloyd Wright: The Collected Writings.* Edited by Bruce Brooks Pfeiffer. Vol. 5. New York: Rizzoli/Frank Lloyd Wright Foundation, 1995.